Covered Bridges of the South
by
Harold Stiver

Table of Contents

Kentucky Covered Bridges

West Virginia Covered Bridges

How to use this Book

For each of the 64 historical or Traditional Covered Bridges remaining in the south, we have included photographs as well as descriptive and statistical data. Traditional Covered Bridges are those that follow the building practices of the Nineteenth Century and the early part of the Twentieth Century or those built later that follow those methods. All of these bridges have had repairs done as portions wear out, and some may have been almost entirely replaced through the years. I have used "The National Society for the Preservation of Covered Bridges, Inc." list of what they consider as Traditional Bridges.

Following is data included for each bridge

Name: This is listed in bold type, and where there are other names, it is the common name or the name listed on an accompanying plaque.

Other Names: Underneath the Common Name in brackets, you will find other names that the bridge has been known by.

Nearest County and Township are listed.

It is frustrating to go on an excursion to see something and not be able to find it. This book offers you multiple ways to ensure that doesn't happen.

GPS Position: This is our recommended method. Enter the coordinates in a good GPS unit and it should take you right there. You, of course, must use care that you are not led off road or on a dangerous route.

Detailed Driving Directions: Directions from a town near to the bridge.

Builder: If known, the name of the original builder(s) is listed.

Year Built: As well as the year built, if it has been moved it will shown with the year preceded by the letter M and, if a major repair has been done, the year will be shown preceded by the letter R.

Truss Type: The type for the particular bridge will be listed. If you are interested in more information on the various types of trusses, access "Truss Types" from the Table of Contents.

Dimensions: The length and number of spans

Notes: A place where you can find additional items of interest about the bridge.

World Index Number:
Covered bridges are assigned a number to keep track of them which consists of three numbers separated by hyphens.

The first number represents the number of the U.S. State in alphabetical order. Following number 50 for the 50th state are additional numbers for Canadian provinces. Thus the numbers 05 represents California.

The second set of numbers represents the county of that state, again based on alphabetical order. Humboldt is the 12th county alphabetically in California, and it is designated as 05-12.

Each bridge in that county is given a number as it was discovered or built. Zane's Ranch was the fifth bridge discovered or built in the County of Humboldt, California and it therefore has the designation of 05-12-05. Sometimes you will see the first set of numbers replaced by the abbreviation for the state, thus CA-12-05.

A bridge is sometimes substantially rebuilt or replaced and it then has the suffix #2 added to it.

National Register of Historic Places: If the bridge has registered, the date is given.

Photographing Covered Bridges
Some standard positions
Portal: Taken to show the ends of bridge or bridge opening. This view, usually symmetrical, will include various signs posted. This is also a good way to get run over, so be careful!

3/4 view: Shows both the front and sides of the bridge, and is often the most attractive.

Side view: Taken from a bank or from the river, this gives not only a nice view of the bridge but usually allows for some interesting foreground elements.

Interior view: An image taken from the interior of the bridge will show some interesting structure but there is not a lot of available light. A tripod is important and HDR processing is helpful.

Landscape View: With the bridge smaller in the frame, you can introduce the habitat around it, particularly effective with colorful autumn foliage.

Using HDR(High Dynamic Range)

HDR is a process where multiple images of varying exposure are combined to make one image.

It has a bad name with some people because many HDR images are super-saturated, a kind of digital age version of an Elvis painted on velvet. However, the process is actually about getting a full range of exposure with no burnt out highlights or blocked shadows. This is an ideal processing solution for photographing Covered Bridges where you often have open light sky set against dark shadowed landscape and structure.

I use a series of three exposures at levels of -1 2/3, 0, +1 2/3, and this normally runs the full exposure range encountered. It is important to use a stable tripod.

One situation where you may need a larger series is shooting from within a bridge and using the window to frame an outside scene. The dynamic range is huge and you will need to have a series with a much larger range.

There are a number of software programs you can use to combine these images including newer editions of Photoshop. I use Photomatix which I have found very versatile and easy to use.

Best times for photographing bridges

Mornings and evenings are generally the best times for outdoor photography but the use of HDR processing makes it easier even in bright direct light. Although any season is good for bridge photography including the winter, fall foliage included in a scene can be spectacular.

A Short History of Covered Bridges

Let's deal with that often posed question; "Why were the bridges covered"
1. Crossing animals thought it was a barn and entered easily. I like this suggestion, it shows imagination. However, its not the answer although the original bridges normally had no windows and this is said to be because animals would not be spooked by the sight of the water.

2. To cover up the unsightly truss structure. I don't think those early pioneers were that sensitive, and personally, I like the look of the trusses.

3. To keep snow off the travelled portion. In fact the bridge owners often paid to have the insides "snowed" in order to facilitate sleighs.

4. It offered some privacy to courting couples, hence "kissing bridges". That is a nice romantic notion but no.

In fact, the bridge was covered for economic reasons. The truss system was where much of the bridge's cost was found, and if left open to the elements, it deteriorated and the bridge became unstable and unsafe. Covering it protected this valuable portion and the roof could be replaced as needed with inexpensive materials and unskilled labour. Without coverings, a bridge might only have a life span of a decade while one that was covered often lasted 75 years or more before repairs became necessary. Besides extending the longevity of a bridge, wooden covered bridges had the virtue that they could be constructed of local materials and there were many available workers skilled in working with wood.

The first known Covered Bridge in North America was built in 1804 by Theodore Burr. It was called the Waterford bridge and it spanned the Hudson River in New York.
For the rest of the century and into the 20th Century, Covered bridge building boomed as the country became populated and people needed to travel between communities. The cost of constructing and maintaining a bridge was normally borne by the nearby community and many bridges charged a toll as a method of offsetting these costs.
The period from 1825 to 1875 was the heyday of bridge building but near the end of that period iron bridges began to supplant them.

The number of Covered bridges may have numbered 10,000 but have now dropped to about 840 spread throughout North America. Many have Historical Designations which provides them protection and many communities are interested in protecting their local historical bridges.

Alabama County Map

Swann (Joy) Covered Bridge
County: Blount, Alabama
Township: Cleveland

GPS Position: N 33° 59.824' W 86° 36.078'
Directions: From the town of Cleveland go west from AL-53/US-231 on Swann Bridge Road for 1.5 miles where you will find the bridge

Crosses: Locust Fork, Black Warrior River
Carries: Swann Bridge Road

Builder: Zelmer C. and Forrest Tidwell
Year Built: 1933 (R1979) (R2012) (R2018) (R2022)
Truss Type: Town
Dimensions: 3 Span, 305 feet

Notes: This is the longest historical Covered Bridge in the Southern Region. It was closed to vehicle traffic in 2009 and re-opened in 2012 after repairs were completed. The 2018 and 2022 repairs were needed due to vehicle accidents. It is currently the longest existing historic covered bridge in Alabama

World Index Number: AL/01-05-05
National Register of Historic Places: August 20, 1981

Hortons Mill Covered Bridge
County: Blount, Alabama
Township: Horton

GPS Position: N 34° 00.455' W 86° 26.918'
Directions: From the town of Oneonta go north on AL-75/2nd Ave. E. for 3.9 miles and turn left onto Covered Bridge Circle where you will see the bridge
Crosses: Calvert Prong
Carries: Covered Bridge Circle

Builder: Talmedge Horton
Year Built: 1934 (R1974) (R2013)
Truss Type: Town
Dimensions: 2 Span, 203 feet

Notes: The bridge is 70 feet above the water, making it the highest over any waterway of any North American Covered Bridge. It was re-opened for one lane traffic in 2013 after repairs were completed for damage due to vandalism in 2007. Following necessary repairs in 2013, the Horton Mill Covered Bridge was reopened to motor vehicle traffic but has subsequently been closed to vehicles again.

World Index Number: AL/01-05-07
National Register of Historic Places: December 29, 1970

Old Easley (Rosa) Covered Bridge
County: Blount, Alabama
Township: Oneota

GPS Position: N 33° 58.265' W 86° 31.106'
Directions: From the town of Oneata, go northwest on AL-53/US-231 for 0.6 miles and turn left on Easley Bridge Road where you will see the bridge in 1.9 miles

Crosses: Calvert Prong, Dub Branch of the Little Warrior River
Carries: Easley Bridge Road

Builder: Zelmer C. Tidwell and Forrest Tidwell
Year Built: 1927 (R2012)
Truss Type: Town
Dimensions: 1 Span, 82 feet

Notes: The bridge was closed for repairs in 2009 but has reopened to single lane traffic after repairs were completed in 2012. Surveillance camera were installed to protect against vandalism. The restoration was completed by Bob Smith Construction of Alabama.

World Index Number: AL/01-05-12
National Register of Historic Places: August 20, 1981

Coldwater (Hughes Mills) Covered Bridge
County: Calhoun, Alabama
Township: Oxford

GPS Position: N 33° 36.466' W 85° 49.003'
Directions: In the town of Oxford, go east on Recreation Drive off Quintard Ave for 0.7 miles and you will find the bridge

Crosses: Inlet of Oxford lake
Carries: Recreation Drive

Builder: Former slave, name not known
Year Built: C.1850 (R1920) (R1974) (R1990) (M1990)
Truss Type: Multiple Kingpost over Town
Dimensions: 1 Span, 63 feet

Notes: The bridge was built by a former slave whose name is unknown in about 1850. The 1930 repairs were due to fire damage. It is the oldest surviving Covered Bridge in Alabama. It originally spanned Coldwater Creek and is currently open to pedestrians only, In 1990, the bridge was fully restored and moved to Oxford Lake Park.

World Index Number: AL/01-08-01
National Register of Historic Places: April 11, 1973

Clarkson (Legg) Covered Bridge
County: Culman, Alabama
Township: Clarkson

GPS Position: N 34° 12.477' W 86° 59.468'
Directions: From the town of Cullman, go west on AL-74/US-278 for 7.4 miles and turn right on County Rd 111/Bethel Battle Ground Rd. In 0.6 miles turn left on County Road 1043 where you will find the bridge in 0.8 miles.

Crosses: Crooked Creek
Carries: County Road 1043

Builder: James Legg
Year Built: 1904 (R1922) (R1975)
Truss Type: Town
Dimensions: 4 Span, 250 feet

Notes: The 1921 repairs were due to flood damage which washed half of the bridge downstream. A steel bridge eventually replaced the Coldwater Covered Bridge in 1974 and it was closed to traffic. Look also for a restored grist Mill and Log Cabin nearby.

World Index Number: AL/01-22-01
National Register of Historic Places: June 25, 1974

Alamuchee (Bellamy) Covered Bridge
County: Sumpter, Alabama
Township: Livingston

GPS Position: N 32° 35.706' W 88° 11.218'
Directions: In the town of Livingston go northwest on Astrid Street off US-11 and after 400 feet, turn right on University Drive where you will see the bridge in 0.4 miles

Crosses: Pond
Carries: University Drive

Builder: William Alexander Campbell Jones
Year Built: 1861 (M1924) (M1971) (R2017)
Truss Type: Town
Dimensions: 1 Plus Span, 82 feet

Notes: The bridge was moved in 1924 to cross Alamuchee Creek and to the present site at the University of Western Alabama in 1971 where it carries only pedestrian traffic. It is one of the oldest covered bridges still existing in Alabama. Additional restoration work was completed in 2017.

World Index Number: AL/01-60-01
National Register of Historic Places: Not listed

Kymulga Covered Bridge
County: Talladega, Alabama
Township: Kymulga Creek

GPS Position: N 33° 20.052' W 86° 17.995'
Directions: From the town of Childersburg go NW on Desoto Caverns Parkway
for 0.5 mi and make a sharp left on Forest Hill Dr. After 0.2 miles turn right on
Grist Mill Rd and drive 3.6 miles where you will see the bridge on a bypassed
section

Crosses: Talladega Creek
Carries: Grist Mill Road (Bypassed Section)

Builder: Not known
Year Built: c.1860 (R1974)
Truss Type: Howe
Dimensions: 1 Span, 105 feet

Notes: The bridge and the nearby Kymulga Mill were restored in 1974. They are
both part of a public park managed by the Childersburg Historic Preservation
Commission. There is an admission charge

World Index Number: AL/01-61-01
National Register of Historic Places: October 29, 1976

Waldo (Riededle Mill) Covered Bridge
County: Greenup, Alabama
Township: Talladega

GPS Position: N 33° 22.596' W 86° 01.586'
Directions: Where's Waldo? From the town of Talladega go southeast Highway
77/Ashland Highway for 5.3 miles where you will see the Old Mill Restaurant.
The bridge is a short distance east on a private road
Crosses: Talladega Creek
Carries: Private road

Builder: Not known
Year Built: c.1858
Truss Type: Howe and Queenpost
Dimensions: 1 Span, 115 feet

Notes: Ask permission to visit the bridge at the Old Mill Restaurant. The
restaurant was formerly the Riddle Mill from which the bridge receives it's
alternate name. Various restoration plans have been discussed but the bridge is
not currently maintained. It is the second oldest surviving covered bridge in the
state.

World Index Number: AL/01-61-02
National Register of Historic Places: Not listed

Alabama Bridge Tour

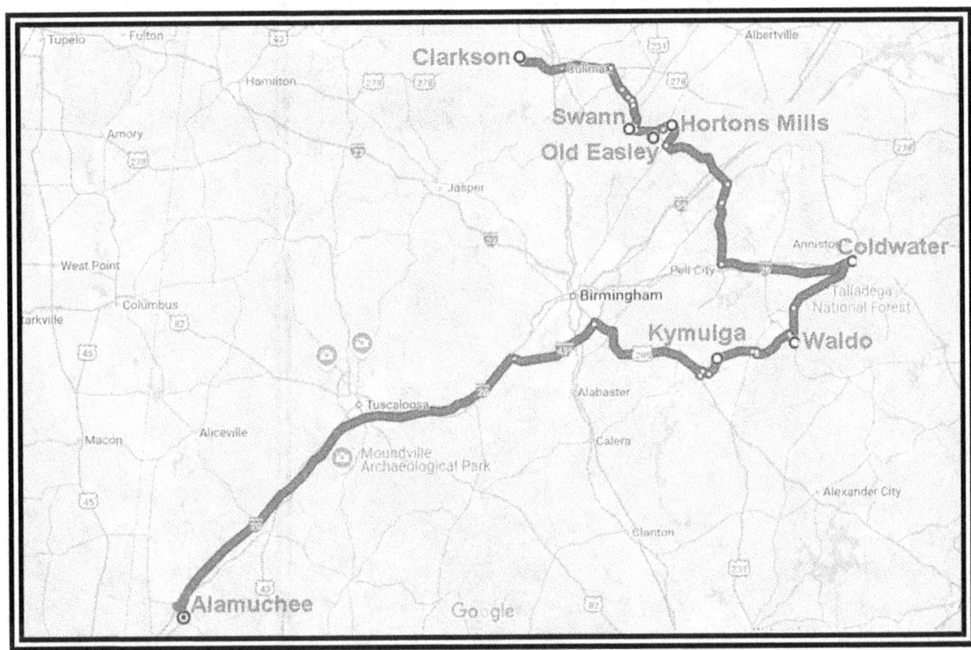

All 8 of Alabama's Historic Covered bridges can be visited in a tour that would
involve some 6 hours of actual driving. This tour run from the northwest towards
the southeast.

Clarkson Covered Bridge	N 34° 12.477' W 86° 59.468'
Swann Covered Bridge	N 33° 59.824' W 86° 36.078'
Old Easley Covered Bridge	N 33° 58.265' W 86° 31.106'
Hortons Mills Covered Bridge	N 34° 00.455' W 86° 26.918'
Coldwater Covered Bridge	N 33° 36.466' W 85° 49.003'
Waldo Covered Bridge	N 33° 22.596' W 86° 01.586'
Kymulga Covered Bridge	N 33° 20.052' W 86° 17.995'
Alamuchee Covered Bridge	N 32° 35.706' W 88° 11.218'

Georgia County Map

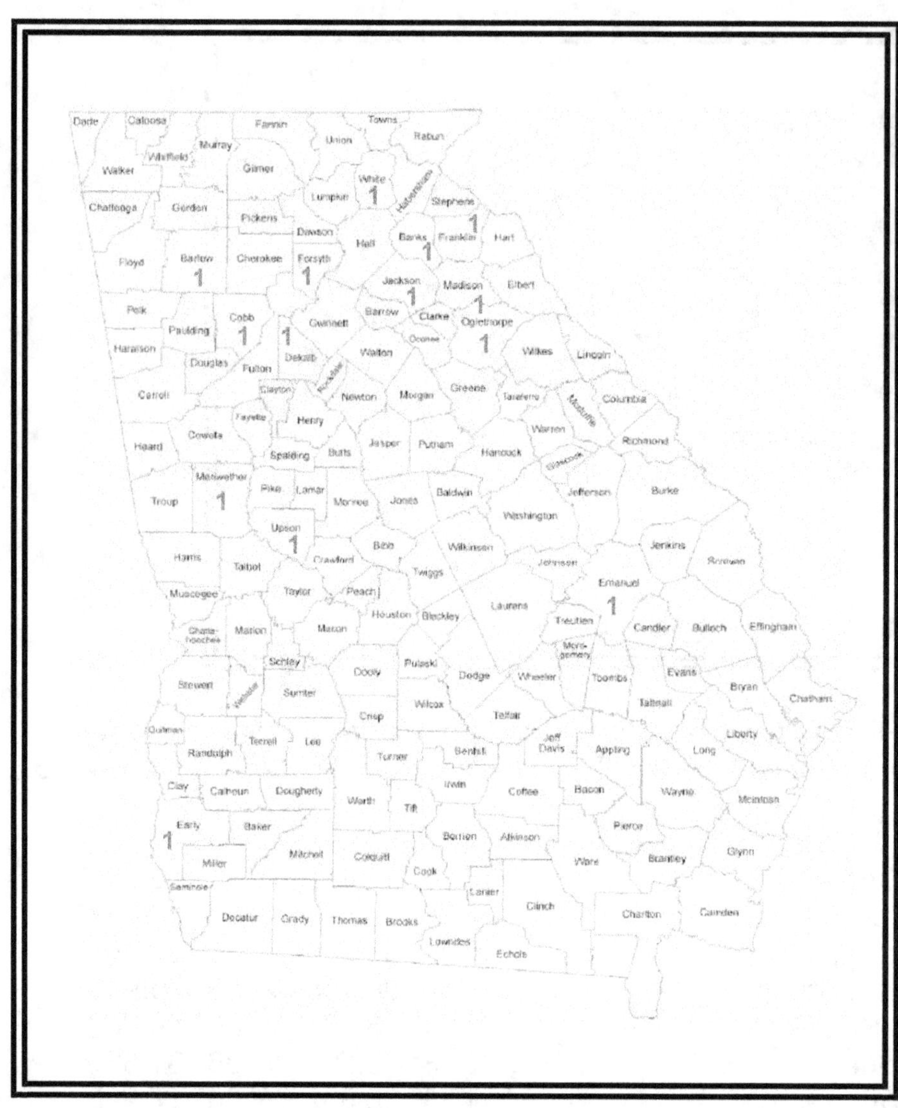

Lula (Blind Susie, Hyder, Garrison) Covered Bridge
County: Banks, Georgia
Township: Lula

GPS Position: N 34° 21.573' W 83° 38.479'
Directions: From the town of Lula, go southeast on GA-51 for 2.1 miles and turn right on Antioch Road where you will find the bridge in 1.0 miles

Crosses: Grove Creek
Carries: Private Road

Builder: Not known
Year Built: 1975
Truss Type: Modified Kingpost
Dimensions: 1 Span 34 feet

Notes: The original bridge was built in 1915 about a mile away but was moved to its present site. It was bypassed in 1969 when Antioch Road was realigned. In 1975, it was dismantled and rebuilt. The bridge is located on private property which is posted but it is easy to view and photograph from Antioch Road

World Index Number: GA/10-06-06#2
National Register of Historic Places: Not listed

Euharlee Creek (Lowry) Covered Bridge
County: Bartow, Georgia
Township: Euharlee

GPS Position: N 34° 08.596' W 84° 55.863'
Directions: From the town of Euharlee, go south on Euharlee Rd/Covered Bridge Rd for 0.2 mi and turn right on Old Covered Bridge Rd SW where the bridge is a short way

Crosses: Euharlee Creek
Carries: Covered Bridge Road (Bypassed Section)

Builder: Washington King and Jonathan H. Burke
Year Built: 1886
Truss Type: Town
Dimensions: 1 Span 138 feet

Notes: The bridge was closed and bypassed in 1980 when a modern two lane bridge was constructed. It hosts a fall Festival in October each year. The bridge was built to service the nearby Lowry Mill where it gets its alternate name. The remains of the mill can be seen. Look also for the 1850s Village exhibit nearby.

World Index Number: GA/10-08-01
National Register of Historic Places: Not listed

Concord (Ruffs Mill, Nickajack Creek) Covered Bridge
County: Cobb, Georgia
Township: Smyrna

GPS Position: N 33° 50.958' W 84° 33.539'
Directions: From Smyrna go south on Hicks Rd from the East-West Connector
for 0.6 miles and turn left on Concord Rd where you will find the bridge in 1.2 mi

Crosses: Nickajack Creek
Carries: Concord Road

Builder: John Wesley Ruff
Year Built: 1872 (R1950s)
Truss Type: Modified Queenpost
Dimensions: 2 span 132 feet

Notes: The work done in the 1950s added steel supports and additional concrete
piers. Like many covered bridges, this one is said to be haunted but the ghosts
here seem to be unique. They are said to be the spirits of drowned children who
will take Snicker bars left on the roofs of cars at night. Ghosts with a sweet tooth.
Look also for the Ruff's Mill nearby.

World Index Number: GA/10-33-02
National Register of Historic Places: March 26, 1976

Stone Mountain (College Avenue, Effie's) Covered Bridge
County: De Kalb, Georgia
Township: Stone Mountain

GPS Position: N 33° 48.215' W 84° 07.996'
Directions: Found in Stone Mountain Park east of the town of Stone Mountain. Head east on Robert E Lee Blvd for 2.0 miles and turn left on Covered Bridge Road where the bridge is a short distance. There is an admission charge for the park

Crosses: Stone Mountain Lake
Carries: Covered Bridge Road

Builder: Washington W. King
Year Built: 1893 (R1911) (M1965)
Truss Type: Town
Dimensions: 1 plus span, 151 feet

Notes: The bridge originally spanned the Oconee River in Clarke County but was purchased for $1 and moved to its present location in 1965. Look also for a riverboat, skylift, museum and zoo.

World Index Number: GA/10-44-01
National Register of Historic Places: Not listed

Coheelee Creek (Hilton) Covered Bridge
County: Early, Georgia
Township: Rock Hill

GPS Position: N 31° 18.372' W 85° 04.711'
Directions: From the town of Blakely go SW on GA-62 for 8.5 miles and turn right on Martin Road. After 0.4 miles, turn right on Old River Road where the bridge is 1.1 miles.

Crosses: Coheelee Creek
Carries: Old River Road

Builder: J.W. Baughman
Year Built: 1891 (R1958) (R1984) (R2003)
Truss Type: Modified Kingpost-Queenpost
Dimensions: 2 spans, 120 feet

Notes: This is the most southern historic Covered Bridge in North America. It is closed to traffic. The concrete abutments were added in 1958. The creek has a waterfall that can make interesting photos

World Index Number: GA/10-49-02
National Register of Historic Places: May 13, 1976

Parrish Mill (Watson Mill) Covered Bridge
County: Emanuel, Georgia
Township: Twin City

GPS Position: N 32° 32.701' W 82° 07.469
Directions: Located in the George L. Smith State Park. From the town of Twin City go south on GA-23 for 2.9 miles and turn left on George L. Smith State Park Road where you will find the bridge site in 1.9 miles.

Crosses: Fifteenmile Creek
Carries: George L. Smith State Park Road

Builder: James Parrish and Alexander Henricks
Year Built: 1880
Truss Type: Post and Beam
Dimensions: 1 plus span, 101 feet

Notes: Essentially this is a mill. It crosses the creek and has doors for pedestrian passage, it also qualifies as a Covered Bridge. The mill still grinds small amounts of cornmeal which can be purchased by visitors. The mill and bridge are unique structures that offer a host of interesting photo opportunities.

World Index Number: GA/10-53-M1
National Register of Historic Places: Not listed

Ducktown (Poole's Mill) Covered Bridge
County: Forsyth, Georgia
Township: Heardville

GPS Position: N 34° 17.459' W 84° 14.537'
Directions: From the town of Ball Ground, go south on GA-372/Ball Ground Rd for 6.0 miles and turn left on GA-369/Hightower Rd. After 3.8 miles turn right on Pooles Mill Road and you will find the bridge in 0.6 miles at Poole's Bridge Park

Crosses: Settendown Creek
Carries: Pooles Mill Road (Bypassed Section)

Builder: John Wofford and Bud Gentry
Year Built: 1906 (R1988)
Truss Type: Town
Dimensions: 1 Span, 94 feet

Notes: The original builder drilled all the holes for the truss members wrong and then abandoned the project. Bud Gentry took over and drilled new holes but the originals can still be seen. The bridge was in poor shape but the repairs in 1988 fixed it up nicely. A support pier was also added at this time.

World Index Number: GA/10-58-01
National Register of Historic Places: April 1, 1975

Cromer's Mill (Nail's Creek) Covered Bridge
County: Franklin, Georgia
Township: Cromer's Mill

GPS Position: N 34° 16.509' W 83° 15.955'
Directions: From the town of Franklin Springs, go west on GA-145/Toccoa Carnesvilles Rd for 1.1 miles and turn left on GA-51/Sandy Cross Road. Drive 4.7 miles and turn left on GA-106/Athens Road and then after 1.5 miles, turn right on Cromers Bridge Road and the bridge is a short distance on a closed section.

Crosses: Nail's Creek
Carries: Cromers Bridge Road (Bypassed Section)

Builder: James Hunt
Year Built: 1906 (R1999)
Truss Type: Town
Dimensions: 1 Span 110 feet

Notes: The bridge had depreciated in condition before the 1999 rehabilitation brought it back to shape. A steel brace was added and some of the top chords replaced.

World Index Number: GA/10-59-01
National Register of Historic Places: August 17, 1976

Hurricane Shoals Covered Bridge
County: Jackson, Georgia
Township: Maysville

GPS Position: N 34° 12.855' W 83° 32.707'
Directions: From Maysville, go south on Georgia 82 Connecter for 2.2 miles and turn left onto Hurricane Shoals Park Road where the bridge is found in a short distance.

Crosses: North Oconee River
Carries: Hurricane Shoals Park Road

Builder: David Roebuck (Architect)
Year Built: 2002 (Original bridge built in 1870)
Truss Type: Town
Dimensions: 3 Spans 128 feet

Notes: The original bridge was burned by vandals on May 31, 1972. This second bridge was opened in 2002 after prodding and hard work by many individuals and organizations. Look also for the reconstructed Gristmill nearby

World Index Number: GA/10-78-01#2
National Register of Historic Places: Not Listed

Watson Mill (Carlton) Covered Bridge
County: Madison and Oglethorpe Counties, Georgia
Township: Grove Creek

GPS Position: N 34° 01.616' W 83° 04.498'
Directions: From Comer, go east on GA-72/Sunset Ave. for 3.6 miles and turn right on Railroad Ave, continuing on Watson Mill, Bridge Rd and Watson Mill Rd where you will find the bridge in 2.0 miles in Watson Mill Bridge State Park.

Crosses: Broad River, South Fork
Carries: Watson Mill Road

Builder: Washington W. King
Year Built: C.1885 (R1971)
Truss Type: Town
Dimensions: 3 Spans, 229 feet

Notes: This is the longest Covered Bridge in Georgia and an excellent park with campsites and shelters has been constructed around it. There are also stalls and trails for horse owners. The bridge was built to service a mill owned by Gabriel Watson. Their are only traces remaining of this mill.

World Index Number: 17-81-01
National Register of Historic Places: 03/26/1976

Red Oak (Imlac) Covered Bridge
County: Meriwether, Georgia
Township: Gay

GPS Position: N 33° 02.305' W 84° 33.129'
Directions: From Woodbury, go north on GA-74/GA-85 for 2.2 mi and turn right on Co Rd 281/Covered Bridge Road where you will see the bridge in 1.2 miles.

Crosses: Red Oak Creek
Carries: Covered Bridge Road

Builder: Horace King
Year Built: c.1840 (R1880s) (R1999)
Truss Type: Town
Dimensions: 1 Span 99 feet

Notes: One of the finest of Georgia's Covered Bridges, it still serves one lane of traffic. The 1999 rehabilitation included a new roof, some of the ceiling beams and truss members and height restrictors at each end. Horace King, born in slavery, constructed dozens of bridges in Alabama, Georgia, and Mississippi

World Index Number: GA/10-77-02
National Register of Historic Places: May 5, 1994

Elder's Mill (Rose Creek) Covered Bridge
County: Oconee , Georgia
Township: Farmington

GPS Position: N 33° 48.153' W 83° 21.819'
Directions: From the town of Watkinsville, go southeast on GA-15/Greensboro Highway for 3.1 miles and turn right on Elder Mill Road where you will find the bridge in 0.8 miles

Crosses: Rose Creek
Carries: Elder Mill Road

Builder: Nathaniel Richardson
Year Built: 1897 (M1924)
Truss Type: Town
Dimensions: 1 Span 99 feet

Notes: The bridge originally crossed Calls Creek on the road between Athens and Watkinsville in 1924. It was moved by wagon to its present location by John Chandler in 1924

World Index Number: GA/10-108-01
National Register of Historic Places: May 5, 1994

Big Clouds Creek (Howard's) Covered Bridge
County: Oglethorpe, Georgia
Township: Smithonia

GPS Position: N 33° 59.152' W 83° 08.011'
Directions: From the town of Colbert, go southeast on Smithonia/Colbert Road for 5.4 miles and turn left onto Chandler Silver Road/Wildwood Lane where you will find the bridge in 0.1 miles. The site can be overgrown

Crosses: Big Clouds Creek
Carries: Chandler Silver Road

Builder: James Hunt and Washington W. King (See notes)
Year Built: 1905 (R1998)
Truss Type: Town
Dimensions: 1 Span, 162 feet

Notes: The original builder is listed as Mr. Hunt which likely refers to James Hunt who built covered bridges in Georgia including the surviving Cromer's Mill Covered Bridge. Some sources credit Washington W. King as well. It was built with convict labor.

World Index Number: GA/10-109-01
National Register of Historic Places: July 1, 1975

Hootenville (Auchumpkee Creek) Covered Bridge
County: Upson , Georgia
Township: Carsonville

GPS Position: N 32° 45.338' W 84° 13.797'
Directions: From the town of Thomaston, go south on GA-3/US-19/Church St.
for 9.4 miles and turn left on Allen Road where the bridge site is 0.8 miles

Crosses: Auchumpkee Creek
Carries: Allen Road

Builder: Arnold Graton
Year Built: 1997 (Original built in 1892)
Truss Type: Town
Dimensions: 1 Span 120 feet

Notes: The original bridge was destroyed by a flood in 1994 and the replacement
was completed in 1997 by Arnold Graton using traditional methods. The
abutments were raised to protect against future floods. It has been bypassed by
a new bridge and is no longer open to vehicle traffic

World Index Number: GA/10-145-02#2
National Register of Historic Places: Not listed

Stovall Mill (Helen, Sautee, Nacoochee) Covered Bridge
County: White, Georgia
Township: Sautee

GPS Position: N 34° 42.698' W 83° 39.458'
Directions: From the town of Sautee, go north on GA-255 for 2.0 miles and turn right to stay on GA-255 and you will find the bridge in 0.3 miles.

Crosses: Chickamauga Creek
Carries: GA-255 (Bypassed Section)

Builder: Will Pardue
Year Built: 1895
Truss Type: Queenpost
Dimensions: 1 Span 36 feet

Notes: This is the smallest bridge in Georgia. It was closed and bypassed in 1959. It replaced an earlier covered bridge which was washed away in a flood in the early 1890s. It was named for Fred Stovall Sr. who operated a number of mills nearby

World Index Number: GA/10-154-03#2
National Register of Historic Places: Not listed

Georgia Tours

Georgia Tour 1

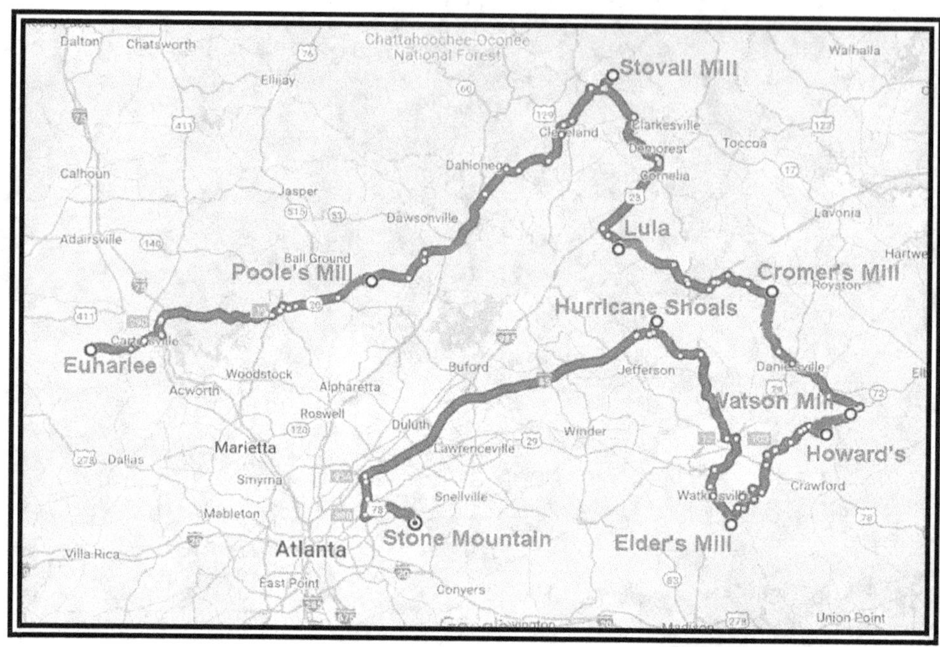

The Georgia Tour #1 drives from west to east and then comes back west. It includes 10 Covered bridges and an estimated driving time of 7 hours.

Euharlee Covered Bridge	N 34° 08.596' W 84° 55.863'
Poole's Mill Covered Bridge	N 34° 17.459' W 84° 14.537'
Stovall Mill Covered Bridge	N 34° 42.698' W 83° 39.458'
Lula Covered Bridge	N 34° 21.573' W 83° 38.479'
Cromer's Mill Covered Bridge	N 34° 16.509' W 83° 15.955'
Watson Mill Covered Bridge	N 34° 01.616' W 83° 04.498'
Howard's Covered Bridge	N 33° 59.152' W 83° 08.011'
Elder's Mill Covered Bridge	N 33° 48.153' W 83° 21.819'
Hurricane Shoals Covered Bridge	N 34° 12.855' W 83° 32.707'
Stone Mountain Covered Bridge	N 33° 48.215' W 84° 07.996'

Georgia Tour 2

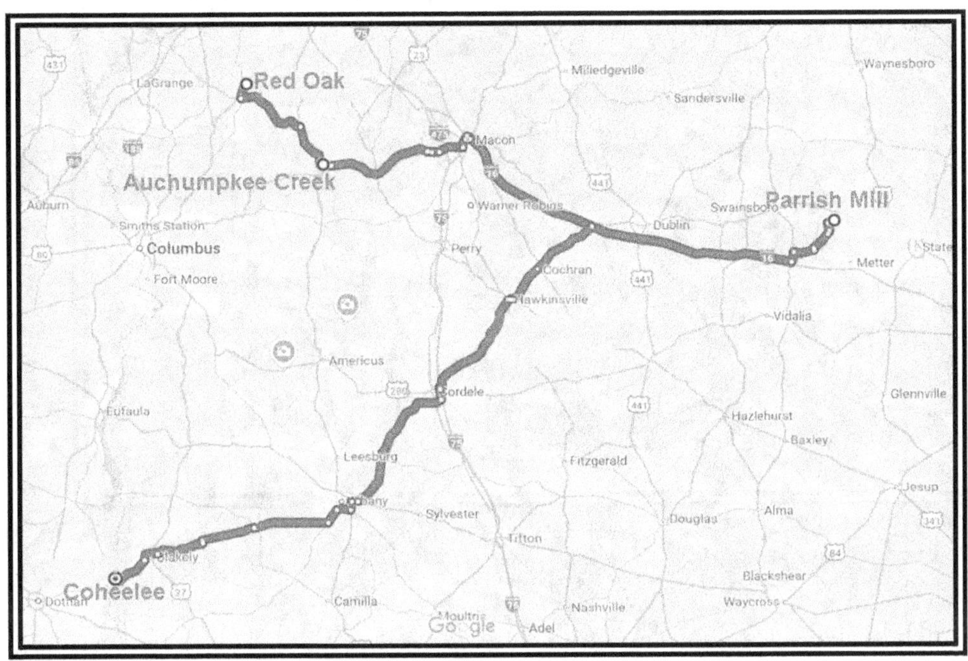

The Georgia Tour 2 involves only 4 covered bridges but they are widely
separated and total driving time is about 7.5 hours.

Red Oak Covered Bridge   N 33° 02.305' W 84° 33.129'
Auchumpkee Creek CB   N 32° 45.338' W 84° 13.797'
Parrish Mill Covered Bridge   N 32° 32.701' W 82° 07.469'
Coheelee Covered Bridge   N 31° 18.372' W 85° 04.711'

Kentucky County Map

Colville Covered Bridge
County: Bourbon, Kentucky
Township: Ruddles Mills

GPS Position: N 38° 19.450' W 84° 12.184'
Directions: From the town of Cynthia, go southeast on KY-32/KY-36/Millersburg
Pike and after 4.5 miles, turn right on Colville Road. You will find the bridge in 2.8
miles.

Crosses: Hinkston Creek
Carries: Colville Rd

Builder: Jacob Bower
Year Built: 2002 (Original built in 1877)
Truss Type: Multiple Kingpost
Dimensions: 1 Span, 120 feet

Notes: The original bridge was built in 1877 and was repaired by Louis Bower in
1913 and by his son, Stock Bower in 1937. The bridge was damaged by a truck
in 1972 and was closed for about a year. It was badly damaged by a flood in
1974 but was rebuilt and re-opened in 2002.

World Index Number: KY/17-09-03#2
National Register of Historic Places: Not listed

Walcott (White) Covered Bridge
County: Bracken, Kentucky
Township: Woolcott

GPS Position: N 38° 43.976' W 84° 05.973'
Directions: From the town of Bladeston, go north on Bladeston Dr for 1 miles and just after Salem Ridge Road, you will see the bridge on a bypassed section of Walcott Rd.\

Crosses: Locust Creek
Carries: Walcott Road (Bypassed)

Builder: Walcott Kennedy built the original bridge in 1824. It was rebuilt in 1881. It was again rebuilt in 2001 after a flood, as it had in 1997 and 1998 and the site was moved 400 feet east, as it was considered safer by the engineers.
Year Built: 2001
Truss Type: Queen and Multiple Kingpost
Dimensions: 1 Span, 76 feet

Notes: The current bridge is not used for vehicle traffic as it was bypassed in 1954. . It is in a nice park like setting. It has been painted white for many years giving it its alternate name.

World Index Number: KY/17-12-01#3
National Register of Historic Places: Not listed

Ringos Mill Covered Bridge
County: Fleming, Kentucky
Township: Flemingburg

GPS Position: N 38° 16.104' W 83° 36.583'
Directions: From the town of Hillsboro go east on KY-128 for 3.5 miles and turn right on Rawlings Road where you will see the bridge in 0.3 miles.

Crosses: Fox Creek
Carries: Bypassed section of KY-158

Builder: Not known
Year Built: 1867 (R1983)
Truss Type: Multiple Kingpost
Dimensions: 1 Span, 86 feet

Notes: This bridge is frequently listed as a Burr Arch construction but it is actually Multiple Kingpost. Like many Kentucky covered bridges, it is unpainted and without windows. It was bypassed in 1968. The name came from a nearby grist mill.

World Index Number: KY/17-35-04
National Register of Historic Places: March 26, 1976

Grange City (Hillsboro) Covered Bridge
County: Fleming County, Kentucky
Township: Grange City

GPS Position: N 38° 15.310' W 83° 39.177'
Directions: From the town of Hillsboro go south on KY-111 for 2.8 miles where you will see the bridge on a section of bypassed road.

Crosses: Fox Creek
Carries: Bypassed section of KY-111

Builder: Not known
Year Built: C.1867 (R2020)
Truss Type: Multiple Kingpost
Dimensions: 1 Span, 86 feet

Notes: This bridge is very similar in construction to the nearby Ringos Mill Covered Bridge and may well have been built by the same unknown builder. It was bypassed in 1968 after a concrete bridge was built upstream from it. In 2020, Arnold Graton Associates added steel supports to stabilize the bridge

World Index Number: KY/17-35-05
National Register of Historic Places: 03/26/1976

Goddard (White) Covered Bridge
County: Fleming, Kentucky
Township: Goddard

GPS Position: N 38° 21.751' W 83° 36.877'
Directions: From the town of Flemingsburg go southeast on KY-32/Water St. for 2.3 miles and turn left to stay on KY-32. After another 5.7 miles turn left on Goddard Bridge Road where you will see the bridge.

Crosses: Sand Lick Creek
Carries: Goddard Bridge Road

Builder: Not known
Year Built: 1864 (M1932) (R1968) (R2006)
Truss Type: Town
Dimensions: 1 Span, 60 feet

Notes: There is a bridge festival here on the fourth Saturday each August. The bridge was originally located one mile south of Goddard but moved here in 1932. It was bypassed 1998. It is the only Kentucky covered bridge to use the Town truss. Similar to other Kentucky Covered bridges, it is unpainted and without windows.

World Index Number: KY/17-35-06
National Register of Historic Places: 08/22/1975

Switzer Covered Bridge
County: Franklin, Kentucky
Township: Switzer

GPS Position: N 38° 15.206' W 84° 45.138'
Directions: From the town of Frankfort go east on US-460 for 1.6 miles and turn left on KY-1262/Switzer Road. In 3.9 miles you will see the bridge on a bypassed section.

Crosses: North Fork Elkhorn Creek
Carries: Bypassed section of KY-1262

Builder: INTECH Engineering (George Hockensmith Original)
Year Built: 1998 (Replaced an original bridge built in 1855)
Truss Type: Howe
Dimensions: 1 Span, 120 feet

Notes: The bridge was rebuilt after being damaged by floods. It is in a lovely quiet setting, a great place for a family picnic. It has been hard hit by graffiti although some consider the messages add to the charm. The outside has not been touched. It was closed to traffic in 1954

World Index Number: KY/17-37-01#2
National Register of Historic Places: Not listed. The original bridge was registered in 09/06/1974

Bennett Mill Covered Bridge
County: Greenup, Kentucky
Township: Lynn

GPS Position: 38°37'50.4"N 82°55'36.6"W
Directions: From the town of Portsmouth go south on KY-7/Main St for 6.1 miles and turn left on Brown Cover Bridge Road where you will see the bridge.

Crosses: Tygarts creek
Carries: Brown Cover Bridge Road

Builder: Brothers Benjamin Franklin Bennett and Parmaly Bennett
Year Built: 2003 (R2003)
Truss Type: Wheeler
Dimensions: 1 Span, 145 feet

Notes: The bridge was built by the Bennetts to provide access to their mill. The historical plaque lists the original construction in 1855 or 1856 but the World Guide to Covered Bridges lists it as 1875. It is the last remaining example of the Wheeler Truss system. It was rebuilt and raised three feet after being damaged in a flood in March 1997.

World Index Number: KY/17-45-01#2
National Register of Historic Places: 03/26/1976

Oldtown Covered Bridge
County: Greenup, Kentucky
Township: Oldtown

GPS Position: N 38° 25.904' W 82° 53.745'
Directions: From the town of Grayson go north on KY-1/Carol Malone Blvd for 8.5 miles and turn right on Frazer Road where you will see the bridge in a short distance.

Crosses: Little Sandy River
Carries: Frazer Road

Builder: INTECH Engineering.
Year Built: 1999 (Original bridge was built in 1880)
Truss Type: Multiple Kingpost
Dimensions: 2 Spans, 190 feet

Notes: The original bridge was closed to traffic in 1985 after a concrete replacement bridge was built nearby. It was rebuilt in 1999 using primarily new materials. It is presently closed to both vehicle and pedestrian traffic.

World Index Number: KY/17-45-02#2
National Register of Historic Places: Not listed (Original bridge was listed 03/26/1976)

Cabin Creek Covered Bridge
County: Lewis, Kentucky
Township: Rectorville

GPS Position: N 38° 36.566' W 83° 37.253'
Directions: From the town of Maysville go east on KY-10/Forest Drive/Mason Lewis Road for 4.5 miles and turn left on KY-984/Springdale Road. After 1.8 miles turn right on KY-984/Cabin Creek Road where you will find the bridge in 2.0 miles.

Crosses: Cabin Creek
Carries: Bypassed section of KY-984

Builder: Mr. Bryant
Year Built: 1873 (R1914) (R1978)
Truss Type: Multiple Kingpost
Dimensions: 1 span, 114 feet

Notes: The bridge was in a very dilapidated condition (see image above) and had a steel framework enclosed to keep it from collapsing. A steel I-beam was added in the 1970s. It was bypassed in 1983. There was funding in place for a restoration and this was done by Arnold Graton in 2013

World Index Number: KY/17-68-03
National Register of Historic Places: 03/26/1976

Dover Covered Bridge
County: Mason, Kentucky
Township: Dover

GPS Position: N 38° 45.028' W 83° 52.726'
Directions: From the town of Dover go south on Lee's Creek Road from KY-8 and you will find the bridge in 0.1 miles.

Crosses: Lee's Creek
Carries: Lee's Creek Road

Builder: Not known
Year Built: C. 1835 (R1912) (R1928) (R1966)
Truss Type: Queenpost
Dimensions: 1 Span, 60 feet

Notes: Like many Kentucky covered bridges, it is unpainted and without windows. A steel stringer has been added for support. It is the oldest covered bridge in Kentucky and one of the oldest in North America. In February 2018, Arnold Grāton Associates stabilized the bridge after flood damage that occurred in 2017.

World Index Number: KY/17-81-01
National Register of Historic Places: 03/26/1976

Johnson Creek Covered Bridge
County: Robertson , Kentucky
Township: Blue Lick Springs

GPS Position: N 38° 28.950' W 83° 58.678'
Directions: From the town of Mt Olivet go east on US-62/Main St for 1.4 miles
and turn right on State Highway 616. After 1.4 miles turn left on Ogden Ridge
Road and after another 2.9 miles, turn right on Old Blue Lick Road. The bridge is
about 0.4 miles.

Crosses: Johnson Creek
Carries: Blue Licks Road

Builder: Jacob N. Bower
Year Built: 1882 (R1912) (R2009)
Truss Type: Bower Isometric
Dimensions: 1 span, 110 feet

Notes: The bridge was damaged by fire in 1910 and was repaired by Jacob's
son, Louis in 1912. The 2009 restoration by Arnold Graton has the structure
looking in top shape although it has attracted graffiti. It was open to traffic after
the restoration, but closed again in 2015

World Index Number: KY/17-101-01
National Register of Historic Places: 09/27/1976

Kentucky Tour

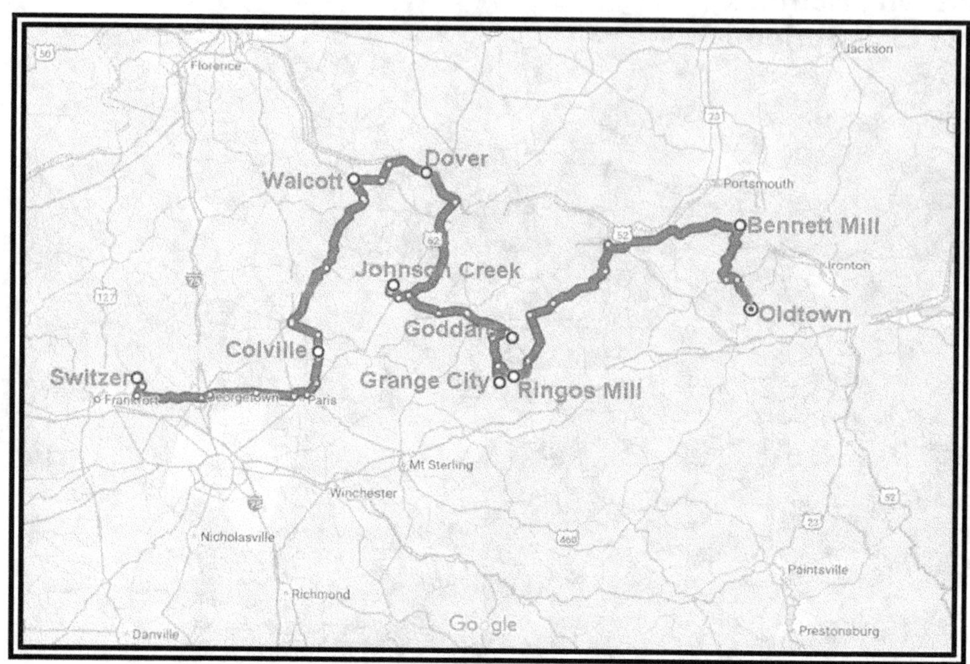

The Kentucky Tour includes 10 bridges and a driving time of 5.5 hours

Switzer Covered Bridge	N 38° 15.206' W 84° 45.138'
Colville Covered Bridge	N 38° 19.450' W 84° 12.184'
Walcott Covered Bridge	N 38° 43.976' W 84° 05.973'
Dover Covered Bridge	N 38° 45.028' W 83° 52.726'
Johnson Creek Covered Bridge	N 38° 28.950' W 83° 58.678'
Goddard Covered Bridge	N 38° 21.751' W 83° 36.877'
Grange City Covered Bridge	N 38° 15.310' W 83° 39.177'
Ringos Mill Covered Bridge	N 38° 16.104' W 83° 36.583'
Bennett Mill Covered Bridge	N 38° 37'50.4" W 82°55'36.6"
Oldtown Covered Bridge	N 38° 25.904' W 82° 53.745'

Missouri County Map

Bollinger Mill Covered Bridge
County: Cape Girardeau, Missouri
Township: Burfordville

GPS Position: 37°22'02.0"N 89°48'09.0"W
Directions: From the town of Burfordville, head east on State Hwy HH for 0.2 miles and turn right onto Bollinger Mill Rd and you will find the bridge in a short distance.

Crosses: Whitewater River
Carries: Bollinger Mill Road

Builder: Joseph Lansmon
Year Built: 1868 (R1908) (R1950) (R1967)
Truss Type: Howe
Dimensions: 1 Span, 140 feet

Notes: Construction of this bridge began in 1860 but was delayed until after the Civil War. The bridge was closed in 1986 due to flood damage. It did not reopen until 1998.

World Index Number: MO/25-16-01
National Register of Historic Places: Listed on the National Register of Historic Places as Bollinger Mill State Historic Site on May 27, 1971

Sandy Creek (LeMay Ferry Road) CB
County: Jefferson, Missouri
Township: Hillsboro

GPS Position: 38°17'38.0"N 90°31'05.0"W
Directions: From the town of Antonia, head southwest on Old Lemay Ferry Road for 5.7 miles and turn left onto Goldman Road. After 0.3 miles, turn left onto Shepherds Way and you will see the bridge

Crosses: Sandy Creek
Carries: Shepherds Way

Builder: John H. Morse
Year Built: 1887 (R1952)
Truss Type: Howe
Dimensions: 1 Span, 76 feet

Notes: The first bridge on this site was built in 1872 but lost to a flood in 1886. The present replacement was constructed by Henry Steffi in 1887 and used portions of the original bridge.

World Index Number: MO/25-50-01#2
National Register of Historic Places: July 8, 1970

Locust Creek Covered Bridge
County: Linn, Missouri
Township: Laclede

GPS Position: 39°47'33.9"N 93°14'20.4"W
Directions: From the town of Meadville, head east on Co Rd Y for 1.7 miles and turn right onto Dart Rd after 1.6 miles you will find the bridge

Crosses: Locust Creek, dry channel
Carries: Dart Rd

Builder: Bishop & Eaton
Year Built: 1868 (R1968) (R1991)
Truss Type: Howe
Dimensions: 1 Span, 151 feet

Notes: At 151 feet, this is the longest surviving covered bridge in Missouri. It was bypassed in 1930. When the channel dried out, the bridge became sitting in mud and in a 1957 report, was found to be in poor condition. In 1991, the bridge was raised six feet to get it off the ground to protect the floor timbers.

World Index Number: MO/25-58-01
National Register of Historic Places: May 19, 1970

Union Covered Bridge
County: Monroe, Missouri
Township: Paris

GPS Position: 39°25'58.0"N 92°06'09.0"W
Directions: From the town of Paris, head west on US-24 BUS W for 1.7 miles
and turn left onto US-24 W. After 3.6 miles, turn left onto State Highway C and go
3.4 miles. Turn right onto State Spur and after 0.4 miles you will see the bridge

Crosses: Elk Fork Salt River
Carries: State Spur

Builder: Joseph C. Elliott
Year Built: 1871 (R1967) (R1988) (R2008) (R2019)
Truss Type: Burr Arch
Dimensions: 1 Span, 125 feet

Notes: The bridge was closed to vehicle traffic in 1970 after being damaged by a
truck. Repairs in 1988 replaced rotted timbers, distorted siding and faulty joints.
The repairs done in 2019 were required after flood damage.

World Index Number: MO/25-69-02
National Register of Historic Places: June 15, 1970

Missouri Tour

This tour of Missouri's 4 covered bridges would involve about 5 hours 45 minutes
of driving

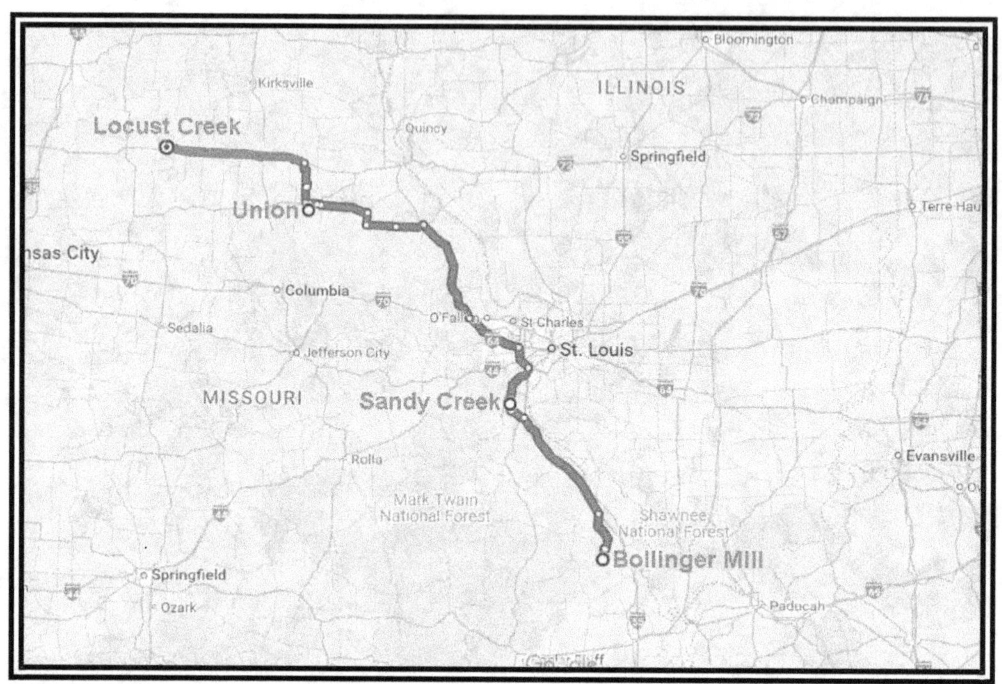

Bollinger Mill Covered Bridge	37°22'02.0"N 89°48'09.0"W
Sandy Creek Covered Bridge	38°17'38.0"N 90°31'05.0"W
Union Covered Bridge	39°25'58.0"N 92°06'09.0"W
Locust Creek Covered Bridge	39°47'33.9"N 93°14'20.4"W

Tennessee County Map

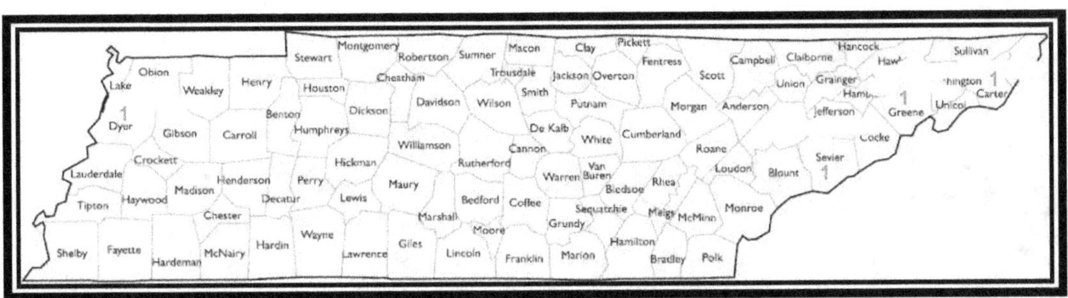

Elizabethton (Doe River) Covered Bridge
County: Carter, Tennessee
Township: Elizabethton

GPS Position: N 36° 20.846' W 82° 12.690'
Directions: Found in the town of Elizabethton on 3rd St between Main St. N and Riverside Dr. N.
Crosses: Doe River
Carries: 3rd St
Builder: E.E. Hunter
Year Built: 1882
Truss Type: Howe
Dimensions: 1 span, 134 feet

Notes: The Elizabethton Covered Bridge Day celebrated every year for a week in June. The builder E.E Hunter was a local doctor who was called upon when a qualified contractor couldn't be found by the County. He called the bridge his "$5 dollar bridge" as he realized that much profit from the job. Available for pedestrian and bicycle traffic over the Doe River it is closed to all motor vehicle traffic

World Index Number: TN/42-10-01
National Register of Historic Places: Elizabethton Historic District includes the bridge site, 03/14/1973.

Emerson E. Parks Farm Covered Bridge
County: Dyer, Tennessee
Township: Trimble

GPS Position: N 36° 12.306' W 89° 11.464'
Directions: Found in the town of Trimble in Park Plaza at the north end of Main Street

Crosses: On dry land
Carries: Park interior

Builder: Emerson E. Parks
Year Built: 1912 (M1997)
Truss Type: Kingpost
Dimensions: 1 span, 33 feet

Notes: This bridge has had an interesting life. It started out as a private bridge which spanned a ditch between two fields. In 1914 it was hit by a tornado which ripped away the gable roof and it was replaced with a flat roof. It was in use until 1928 but remained on the farm until it was relocated to its present site in 1997. It is the only one in the western portion of the state

World Index Number: TN/42-23-01
National Register of Historic Places: Not listed

Bible (Chucky) Covered Bridge
County: Greene, Tennessee
Township:
Warrenburg

GPS Position: N 36° 07.468' W 83° 03.179'
Directions: Head onto TN-340 N from Parrotsville for 7.6 mi and turn right onto Bewley Rd. After 1.4 mi turn left onto State Hwy 349 and after 0.9 mi turn right onto Bible Branch Rd and the bridge is on the left

Crosses: Little Chucky Creek
Carries: Bible Branch Rd (Bypassed section)

Builder: A.A. McLean
Year Built: 1922 or 1923 (R1973)
Truss Type: Queenpost
Dimensions: 1 span, 57 feet

Notes: The bridge was privately built on a farm but in 1940 the county bought the structure from Mr. Bible and it became a public bridge. Originally it was unpainted and without windows, in 1973 the bridge was rehabilitated and had small windows added and was painted red.

World Index Number: TN/42-30-01
National Register of Historic Places: Not listed

Pigeon (Harrisburg) Covered Bridge
County: Sevier, Tennessee
Township: Harrisburg

GPS Position: N 35° 51.646' W 83° 28.965'
Directions: From Sevierville go east on E Main St for 0.4 mi and continue onto Hwy 411 N/Dolly Parton Pkwy. After 3.4 mi, turn right onto TN-339 E and drive 0.9 mi and turn right onto Harrisburg Rd. In 0.2 mi turn right to stay on Harrisburg Rd. where you will find the bridge..
Crosses: Little Pigeon River, East Fork
Carries: Harrisburg Rd

Builder: Elbert Stephenson Early
Year Built: 1875 (R1952) (R1972) (R1983) (R2004)
Truss Type: Queenpost
Dimensions: 1 span, 64 feet

Photo Tip: The sides are posted but there is access from the north corner which yields the best view.
Notes: The bridge is said to have had a concrete pier added in 1952 but recent renovations have removed it and the bridge closer to its original condition.

World Index Number: TN/42-78-01
National Register of Historic Places: 06/10/1975

Tennessee Tour

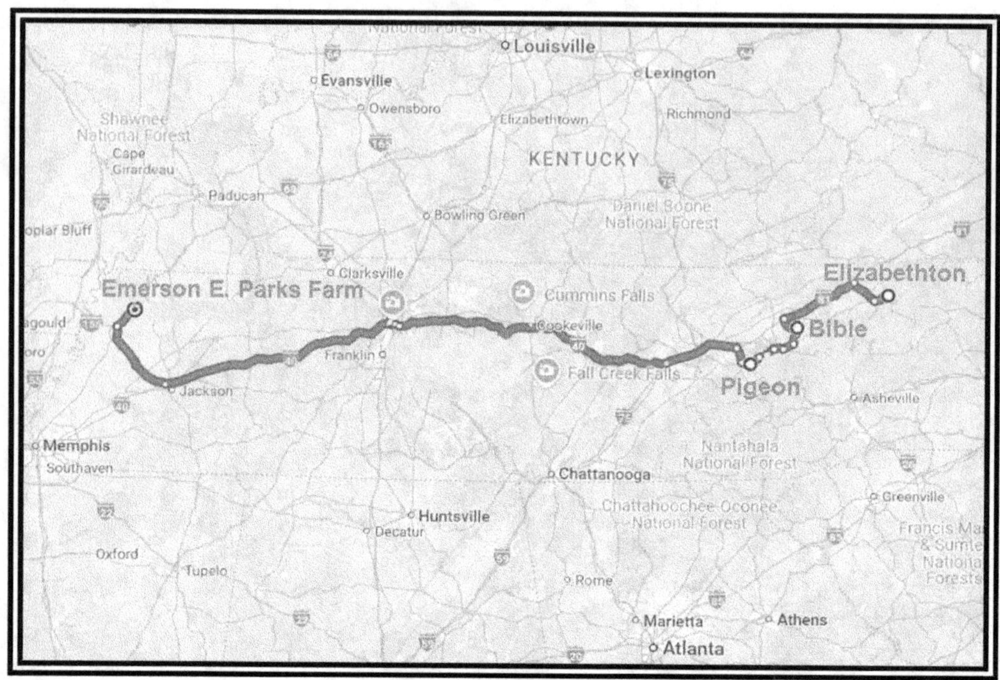

The 3 eastern bridges involve about 2.5 hours of driving. Emerson E. Parks Farm Covered Bridge, the only western site, is an additional 6 hours driving time.

Elizabethton Covered Bridge	N 36° 20.846' W 82° 12.690'
Bible Covered Bridge	N 36° 07.468' W 83° 03.179'
Pigeon Covered Bridge	N 35° 51.646' W 83° 28.965'
Emerson E. Parks Farm CB	N 36° 12.306' W 89° 11.464'

Virginia County Map

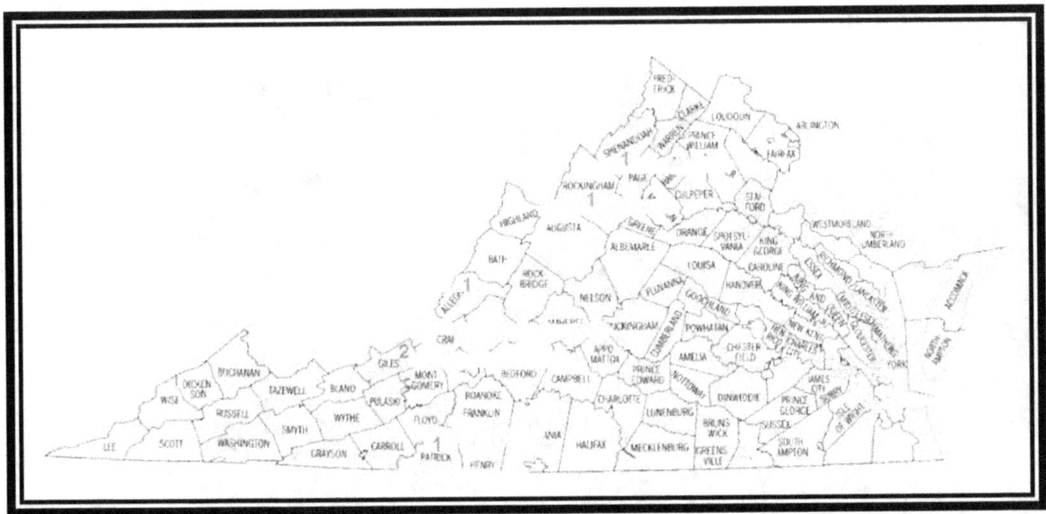

Humpback Covered Bridge
County: Alleghany, Virginia
Township: Covington

GPS Position: N 37° 48.017' W 80° 02.847'
Directions: From US-60 1.2 miles east of junction with I-64, go right on VA-600 for a short distance where you will see a park which is the site of the bridge.
Crosses: Dunlap Creek
Carries: Park road

Builder: James River
Year Built: 1857 (R1954)
Truss Type: Multiple Kingpost Trussed Arch
Dimensions: 1 span, 100 feet

Notes: A unique bridge with the humpbacked appearance from building the center 4 feet highers than the portals. This may have been meant to prevent damage from floods. It was closed in 1929 when a steel truss bridge was built adjacent to it. The covered bridge stood derelict until it was restored in 1954 through the efforts of local organizations and now is a popular exhibit. It is a magnet for photographers, showing picturesque views from all sides.

World Index Number: VA/46-03-01
National Register of Historic Places: October 1, 1969

Sinking Creek Covered Bridge
County: Giles, Virginia
Township: Newport

GPS Position: N 37° 18.403' W 80° 29.875'
Directions: From the town of Blacksburg go north on US-460and after 4.9 miles turn right on VA-42 and then after 1.0 miles turn left on VA-601. You will see the bridge on a bypassed section in about 0.7 miles
Crosses: Sinking Creek
Carries: VA-601 (Bypassed Section)

Builder: Not known
Year Built: 1916 (R2000)
Truss Type: Segmented tied arch
Dimensions: 1 Span, 70 feet

Notes: When the bridge was bypassed by a concrete bridge in 1963, it was left in place but it wasn't until 1995 that the county of Giles claimed ownership. There are paving stones near the portal which record the names of contributors to the 2000 restoration. It is not in the National Register of Historic Places although it is likely eligible. The memorial paving stones and flag offers photographers some nice elements for compositions.

World Index Number: VA/46-35-01
National Register of Historic Places: Not Listed

Link's Farm Covered Bridge
County: Giles, Virginia
Township: Newport

GPS Position: N 37° 18.641' W 80° 30.996'
Directions: From the town of Newport go north on US-460 for 1.6 miles and turn right on VI-700. After 0.2 miles you will make a slight left on Covered Bridge Lane where you will see the bridge.
Crosses: Sinking Creek
Carries: VA-700 (Bypassed Section)

Builder: James Puckett
Year Built: 1912 (R1995)
Truss Type: Segmented tied arch
Dimensions: 1 Span, 49 feet

Notes: The bridge is on private property and is still in use by the owner. You need to obtain permission to visit it. However, it is easy to view and photograph from the public road.

World Index Number: VA/46-35-02
National Register of Historic Places: Not Listed

Jack's Creek (Upper) Covered Bridge
County: Patrick, Virginia
Township: Woolwine

GPS Position: 36°45'52.1"N 80°16'25.4"W
Directions: From the town of Woolwine, head east on VA-8 S for 2.3 miles and turn right onto State Rte 615 where the bridge is 0.1 miles.
Crosses: Smith River
Carries: Va-615 (Bypassed section)

Builder: Charles Vaughan
Year Built: 1916 (R1969) (R1974)
Truss Type: Queenpost
Dimensions: 1 Span, 48 feet

Notes: The bridge was named for the nearby Jack's Creek primitive Baptist Church which it was built to provide access. Patrick County has a bridge festival every June which includes activities at this bridge. The interior has diagonal wood sheaths which covers the truss and make interior images interesting. It was bypassed in 1932.

World Index Number: VA/46-68-02
National Register of Historic Places: May 22, 1973

Biedler Farm Covered Bridge
County: Rockingham, Virginia
Township: Plains

GPS Position: N 38° 35.005' W 78° 42.666'
Directions: From I-81 Exit 264 it is northeast for 2.4 miles and then o.5 miles on a private road.
Crosses: Smith Creek
Carries: Private lane

Builder: Daniel Ulrich Biedler
Year Built: 1896 (R1989)
Truss Type: Burr arch
Dimensions: 1 Span, 92 feet

Notes: The bridge is on private property and you need to obtain permission to visit it.

World Index Number: VA/46-79-01
National Register of Historic Places: Not listed

Meem's Bottom Covered Bridge
County: Shenandoah, Virginia
Township: Mount Jackson

GPS Position: N 38° 43.238' W 78° 39.254'
Directions: From I-81 take exit 269 east on Caverns Rd/State Route 730 for 0.8 miles and turn left on US-11/Old Valley Pike. In 0.9 miles go left on State Road 70/Wissler Road where bridge is a short distance.

Crosses: North Fork of the Shenandoah River
Carries: State Road 70/Wissler Road

Builder: John W. B. Woods
Year Built: 1894 (R1979)
Truss Type: Multiple Kingpost and Burr arch
Dimensions: 4 spans including 3 added concrete piers, 203 feet

Notes: This bridge was burned by vandals 1976 and was salvaged and restored in 1979. In 1983 after a floor beam broke it was repaired and the piers as well as steel i-beams were added. It still carries traffic. There is a nice panoramic side view.

World Index Number: VA/46-82-01
National Register of Historic Places: June 10, 1975

Virginia Bridge Tour

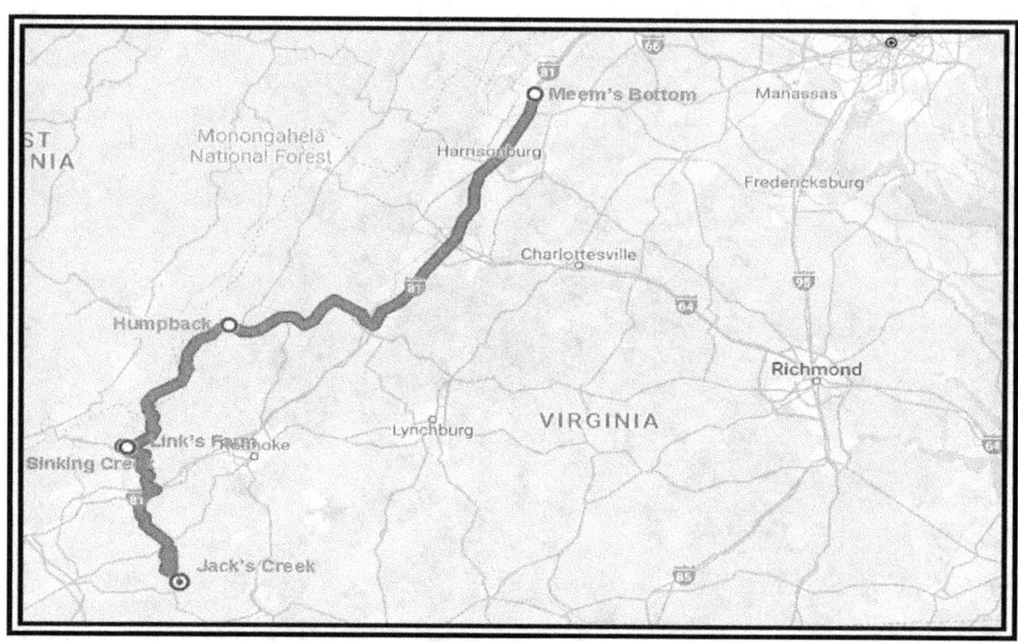

5 of Virginia's Historic Covered Bridges can be visited in a tour that would involve some 4.5 hours of actual driving. This tour run from the northeast towards the southwest.

Meems Bottom Covered Bridge	N 38° 43.238' W 78° 39.254'
Humpback Covered Bridge	N 37° 48.017' W 80° 02.847'
Link's Farm Covered Bridge	N 37° 18.641' W 80° 30.996'
Sinking Creek Covered Bridge	N 37° 18.403' W 80° 29.875'
Jack's Creek Covered Bridge	N 36° 45.868' W 80° 16.423'

West Virginia County Map

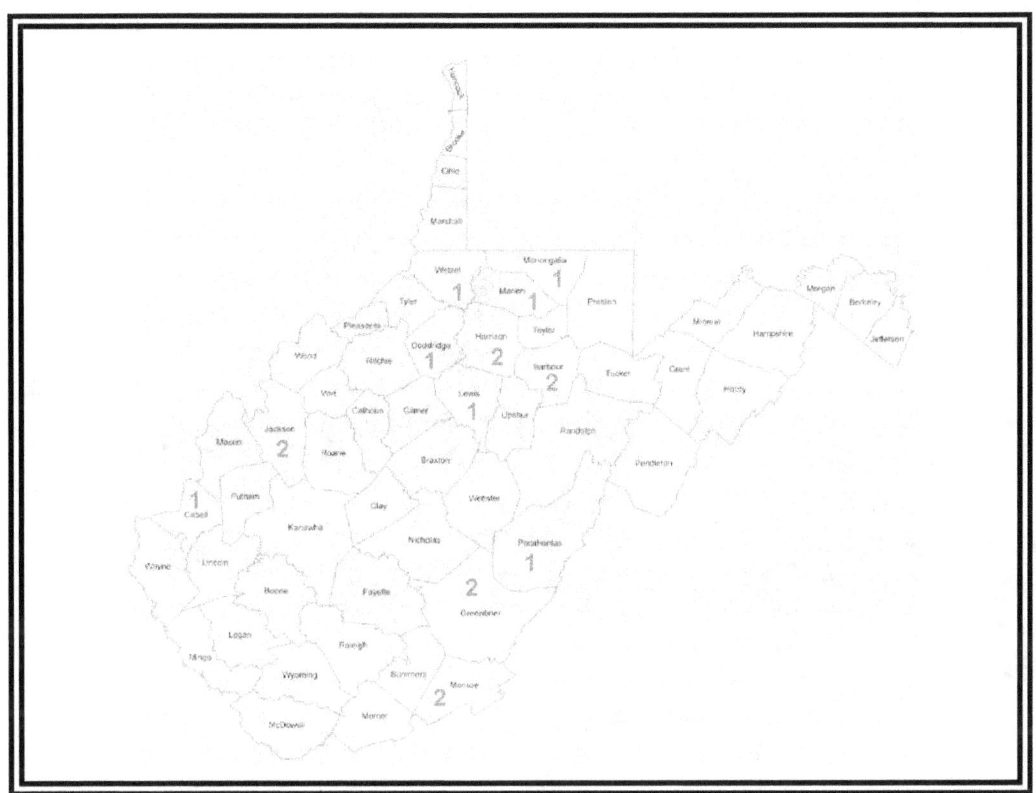

Phillippi Covered Bridge
County: Barbour, West Virginia
Township: Phillippi

GPS Position: N 39° 09.217 W 80° 02.561'
Directions: In the town of Phillippi, it is on Main St. N just east of the intersection of US-119
Crosses: Tygart Valley River
Carries: North Main Street
Builder: Lemuel Chenoweth
Year Built: 1852 (R1934) (R1991)
Truss Type: Burr Variation
Dimensions: 4 Spans (2 Piers have been added), 304 feet

Notes: This is a magnificent structure with two active lanes of traffic (double-barrelled) and a pedestrian walkway. It was used by both the North and South during the Civil War but thankfully neither side burnt it, as was the fate of many other bridges in that period. In 1989, the bridge was accidentally burned when gasoline from a nearby station leaked on the bridge and set it alight. By 1991, the structure was restored to service.

World Index Number: WV/48-01-01
National Register of Historic Places: September 14, 1972

Carrollton Covered Bridge
County: Barbour, West Virginia
Township: Union

GPS Position: N 39° 05.423' W 80° 05.220'
Directions: From the town of Phillippi go south on US-119 for 5.0 km and turn left on Carrolton Road/ CR-36 where you will find the bridge in 0.7 miles

Crosses: Buckhannon River
Carries: Carrolton Road/ CR-36

Builder: Daniel and Emmett J. O'Brien
Year Built: 1856 (R1962) (R2002) (2017)
Truss Type: Burr arch
Dimensions: 1 Span (+2 concrete piers added), 156 feet

Notes: This bridge still carries traffic and is in beautiful shape after the 2002 rehabilitation. In 1962 steel i-beams and two concrete piers were added to strengthen the structure. It was damaged by fire in 2017

World Index Number: WV/48-01-02
National Register of Historic Places: June 4, 1981

Milton (Sink's Mill) Covered Bridge
County: Cabell, West Virginia
Township: Milton

GPS Position: N 38° 25.717' W 82° 07.972'
Directions: In Milton head south on Bill Blenko Dr toward Midland Trail for 0.5 mi. Turn left and it becomes James River Turnpike RdAfter0.1 mi, take a slight left onto Pumpkin Way where the bridge is 0.1 mi.
Crosses: Pond
Carries: None

Builder: R. H. Baker
Year Built: 1876 (R1971) (M2003)
Truss Type: Howe and Arch
Dimensions: 1 Span, 114 feet

Photo Tip: Easy from all sides and a nice reflection on the pond.
Notes: The bridge originally spanned the Mud River but was disassembled in 1977 and remained that way until it was re-assembled at its present site in 2003. It was bypassed for vehicle traffic at this point and restricted to pedestrian use. It was damaged by fire in 2017

World Index Number: WV/48-06-01
National Register of Historic Places: June 10, 1975

Center Point Covered Bridge
County: Doddridge, West Virginia
Township: Center Point

GPS Position: N 39° 23.384' W 80° 38.051'
Directions: From the town of Wallace go west on Rinehart-Little Tenmile and continue on Pike Fork and you will see the bridge in 9.4 miles
Crosses: Pike Fork of McElroy Creek
Carries: Pike Fork Road (Bypassed Section)

Builder: (Carpenters) John Ash and S.H. Smith, (Masons) T.C. Ancell and E. Underwood
Year Built: 1888 or 1890 (R1982) (R2002)
Truss Type: Multiple Kingpost
Dimensions: 1 Span, 43 feet

Notes: The bridge carried public traffic until 1940 when it became privately owned. In 1981 it was donated to the Doddridge County Historical Society. In 1982 it was restored by volunteers. The structure underwent extensive renovations by The Righter Co., Inc. in 2002.

World Index Number: WV/48-09-01
National Register of Historic Places: August 29, 1983

Hern's Mill Covered Bridge
County: Greenbrier, West Virginia
Township: Lewisburg

GPS Position: N 37° 49.951' W 80° 30.263'
Directions: From the town of Lewisberg, go west on Midland Trail and after 2.4 miles turn left on CR-60/11 and after another 0.2 miles go left on CR-40/Hern's Mill Rd where you will find the bridge in 0.8 miles

Crosses: Milligan's Creek
Carries: Hern's Mill Rd

Builder: Not known
Year Built: 1884 (R1962) (R2000)
Truss Type: Queenpost
Dimensions: 1 Span, 54 feet

Notes: Concrete abutment caps and I-beam stringers were added in the rebuild in 2000 performed by Grandview Construction, Inc. The narrow bridge still carries vehicle traffic. The bridge was originally built to provide access to the Hern's Mill as well as local homeowners.

World Index Number: WV/48-13-01
National Register of Historic Places: June 4, 1981

Hokes Mill Covered Bridge
County: Greenbrier, West Virginia
Township: Irish Corner

GPS Position: N 37° 41.871' W 80° 31.517'
Directions: From the town of Ronceverte go southeast on CR-48/River Road
from US-19 and continue on CR-62/Hoke's Mill Rd and after 5.1 miles you will
reach the bridge.

Crosses: Second Creek
Carries: Hoke's Mill Rd (Bypassed Section)

Builder: B.F. Mann, R.A. McDowell and Austin B. Erwin
Year Built: 1899 (R2001)
Truss Type: Long
Dimensions: 1 Span,82 feet

Notes: Built to access the Hoke's Mill, it was closed to traffic in 1991. In 2001, it
was dismantled, repaired and reassembled by Allegheny Restoration, which has
the structure looking great.

World Index Number: WV/48-13-02
National Register of Historic Places: June 4, 1981

Fletcher Covered Bridge
County: Harrison, West Virginia
Township: Ten Mile

GPS Position: N 39° 18.319' W 80° 28.823'
Directions: From the village of Wolf Summit go west on US-50 for 1.7 miles and turn right on Cr-5/Marshville Rd and after 1.6 miles you will see the bridge on CR-5/29

Crosses: Ten Mile Creek
Carries: CR-5

Builder: Soloman Swiger (Abutments L.E. Sturm)
Year Built: 1891 or 1892 (R2002)
Truss Type: Multiple Kingpost
Dimensions: 1 Span, 62 feet

Notes: Named after a nearby family, the bridge is still in use. The original tin roof was replaced in the 2002 restoration by Allegheny Restorations & Bldrs, Inc.. Truss, deck and siding repairs were also completed

World Index Number: WV/48-17-03
National Register of Historic Places: June 4, 1981

Simpson Creek (Holland's Mill, W.T. Law) Covered Bridge
County: Harrison, West Virginia
Township: Simpson

GPS Position: N 39° 18.499' W 80° 16.763'
Directions: From Bridgeport take exit 121 off I-91 onto Meadowbrook Rd east
and shortly turn left onto CR-24/2 where you will see the bridge on a bypassed
section.
Crosses: Simpson Creek
Carries: CR-24/2 (Bypassed section)

Builder: Asa Hugill
Year Built: 1881 (M1888) (R2002)
Truss Type: Multiple Kingpost
Dimensions: 1 Span, 79 feet

Notes: The bridge was originally located a half a mile upstream and after being
washed off its abutments by a 1888 flood, it was situated at its present location.
In 2002, Allegheny Restoration and Builders, Inc. of Morgantown completed a
restoration to replace deteriorated wood in the structure which has the bridge
looking great

World Index Number: WV/48-17-12
National Register of Historic Places: June 4, 1981

Sarvis Fork (New Era) Covered Bridge
County: Jackson, West Virginia
Township: Ravenswood

GPS Position: N 38° 55.294' W 81° 38.697'
Directions: From the town of Sandyville go northeast on Parkersburg Road from Cr-21 for 1.3 miles and turn right on Sarvis Fork Road where you will find the bridge

Crosses: Left Fork of Sandy Creek
Carries: Sarvis Fork Road

Builder: R.C. Construction Co. (George W. Staats Original bridge)
Year Built: 2000 (Replacement of a 1889 bridge)
Truss Type: Long and arch
Dimensions: 1 Span, 102 feet

Notes: The original 1889 bridge was located near Angerona, West Virginia and it was moved to the present site in 1924. The 2000 rebuild by R.C. Construction Co. restored the floor system with a timber deck on steel stringers, installed a stainless steel roof and replaced wooden siding.

World Index Number: WV/48-18-01#2
National Register of Historic Places: Not listed

Staat's Mill Covered Bridge
County: Jackson, West Virginia
Township: Ripley

GPS Position: N 38° 47.660' W 81° 41.212'
Directions: In the town of Ripley at the south end, enter the Cedar Lakes
Conference Center off Old US-21/ Cefar Lake

Crosses: Pond
Carries: None

Builder: H.T. Hartley
Year Built: 1888 (M1983)
Truss Type: Long
Dimensions: 1 Span, 101 feet

Notes: The bridge was originally three miles from the present site at the Tug
Fork of the Bog Mill Creek and was named for Enoch Staat's mill. The bridge was
relocated to the Cedar Lakes FFA-FHA Conference Center as part of a flood
control project in 1983. Situated across one of the conference center's ponds, it
serves pedestrians at the center.

World Index Number: WV/48-18-04
National Register of Historic Places: May 29, 1979

Old Red (Walkersville) Covered Bridge
County: Lewis, West Virginia
Township: Settlement

GPS Position: N 38° 51.511' W 80° 27.615'
Directions: Found just south of Walkersville, take US-19 about 1.0 mile and turn right on Covered Bridge Rd where you will see the bridge

Crosses: Right Fork of West Fork River
Carries: Covered Bridge Rd

Builder: John G. Sprigg
Year Built: 1902 (R1963) (R2003)
Truss Type: Queenpost
Dimensions: 1 Span, 38 feet

Notes: A small but beautiful bridge found in a quiet setting. In August 2002 a major restoration contract was budgeted to replace the wooden siding and deteriorated timbers members. It was awarded to Allegheny Restoration and Builders, Inc. and the work was completed two years later.

World Index Number: WV/48-21-03
National Register of Historic Places: June 4, 1981

Barracksville Covered Bridge
County: Marion, West Virginia
Township: Fairmont

GPS Position: N 39° 30.340' W 80° 10.077'
Directions: Found at the north end of the town of Barracksville on a bypassed section of CR-250 at the intersection of Pike St. And Pine Grove Road

Crosses: Buffalo Creek
Carries: CR-250 (Bypassed section)

Builder: Eli and Lemuel Chenoweth
Year Built: 1853 (R1934) (R1951) (R2000)
Truss Type: Multiple Kingpost and Burr arch
Dimensions: 1 span, 145 feet

Notes: The bridge looks excellent after the 2000 work which involved replacing deteriorated wooden timbers, a new deck and repairs to the roof. The bridge was saved from destruction by Confederate soldiers when the local farm family gave them food in exchange for it's safety. The bridge has been closed to vehicle traffic.

World Index Number: WV/48-25-02
National Register of Historic Places: March 30, 1973

Dent's Run (Laurel Point) Covered Bridge
County: Monongalia, West Virginia
Township: Grant

GPS Position: N 39° 37.432' W 80° 02.452'
Directions: Found west of the town of Morgantown, go west on US-19 for 2.6 miles and turn right on Sugar Grove Road. After 0.6 miles turn left on CR-43/John Fox Road where you will find the bridge on a bypassed section in 0.2 miles
Crosses: Dent's Run
Carries: CR-43 (Bypassed section)

Builder: William and Joseph Mercer, (Abutments) W.Y. Loar
Year Built: 1889 (R1984) (R2004)
Truss Type: Kingpost
Dimensions: 1 span, 40 feet

Notes: Found in a quiet setting, this small bridge is in excellent shape. The bridge was restored in 2004 by Hoke Brothers Contracting, Inc. The work involved repairing the deck and the trusses.

World Index Number: WV/48-31-03
National Register of Historic Places: June 4, 1981

Laurel Creek (Lilydale, Arnott) Covered Bridge
County: Monroe, West Virginia
Township: Springfield

GPS Position: N 37° 33.680' W 80° 37.573'
Directions: From Union go southeast on US-219/Koontz Rd for 2.7 miles and turn right on CR-219/7. In 2.7 miles make a slight right on Cr-23/Laurel Creek Rd and then after 2.8 miles turn left on CR-219/Laurel Creek Rd where you will find the bridge in 0.9 miles
Crosses: Laurel Creek
Carries: Laurel Creek Road

Builder: Charles Robert Arnott, (Abutments) Lewis Miller
Year Built: 1911 (R2000)
Truss Type: Queenpost
Dimensions: 1 Span, 25 feet

Photo Tip: Good from all sides including a creek level side view from the west
Notes: At 25 feet, this is West Virginia's shortest bridge. The bridge was renovated by Hoke Brothers in 2000. At that time a steel deck, installed in 1976, was removed. The structure looks to be in great shape

World Index Number: WV/48-32-01
National Register of Historic Places: June 4, 1981

Indian Creek (Salt Sulphur Springs) Covered Bridge
County: Monroe, West Virginia
Township: Springfield

GPS Position: N 37° 32.814' W 80° 34.498'
Directions: From the town of Union go southwest on South St and continue on US-219/Koontz Rd where you will find the bridge after 4.4 miles

Crosses: Indian Creek
Carries: US-219 (Bypassed section)

Builder: Oscar and Ray Weikel
Year Built: 1903 (R1965) (R2000)
Truss Type: Long
Dimensions: 1 Span, 51 feet

Notes: A great looking bridge with its chocolate colored sides set off by the trees behind it. The builders were said to be 16 and 18 years old at the time of construction. The bridge was bypassed in 1929. The roof and deck were replaced in 2000 by Hoke Brothers Construction.

World Index Number: WV/48-32-02
National Register of Historic Places: April 1, 1975

Denmar (Locust Creek) Covered Bridge
County: Pocahontas, West Virginia
Township: Little Levels

GPS Position: N 38° 04.754' W 80° 14.992'
Directions: From the town of Hillsboro go west on US-219 for 1.8 miles and turn left on Locust Creek Road and then after 3.1 miles turn right on CR-31/Denmar Road where you will see the bridge.

Crosses: Locust Creek
Carries: CR-31/Denmar Road (Bypassed section)

Builder: R.N. Bruce
Year Built: 1870 or 1888 (R1904) (R2001)
Truss Type: Smith Triple
Dimensions: 1 Span, 118 feet

Photo Tip: Excellent all sides including a side view from the new bridge.
Notes: There are no windows in this great looking brown sided bridge. In 2001, Orders Construction Company, Inc. fulfilled a contract to renovate the structure. This included restoring the building as a single-lane pedestrian structure.

World Index Number: WV/48-38-01
National Register of Historic Places: June 4, 1981

Hundred (Fish Creek) Covered Bridge
County: Wetzel, West Virginia
Township: Hundred

GPS Position: N 39° 40.363' W 80° 27.122'
Directions: From the east side of the village of Hundred take CR-1/3 south from US-250 and you will see the bridge.

Crosses: Fish Creek
Carries: CR-1/3

Builder: Lone Pine Construction, Inc.
Year Built: 2001 (Replaced the original bridge from 1881)
Truss Type: Kingpost
Dimensions: 1 Span, 36 feet

Notes: The rebuilt bridge used 4 timber braces from the old bridge but was otherwise built with new material and used steel stringers along with the kingpost trusses. It continues to support vehicle traffic.

World Index Number: WV/48-52-01#2
National Register of Historic Places: Not listed

West Virginia Tour1

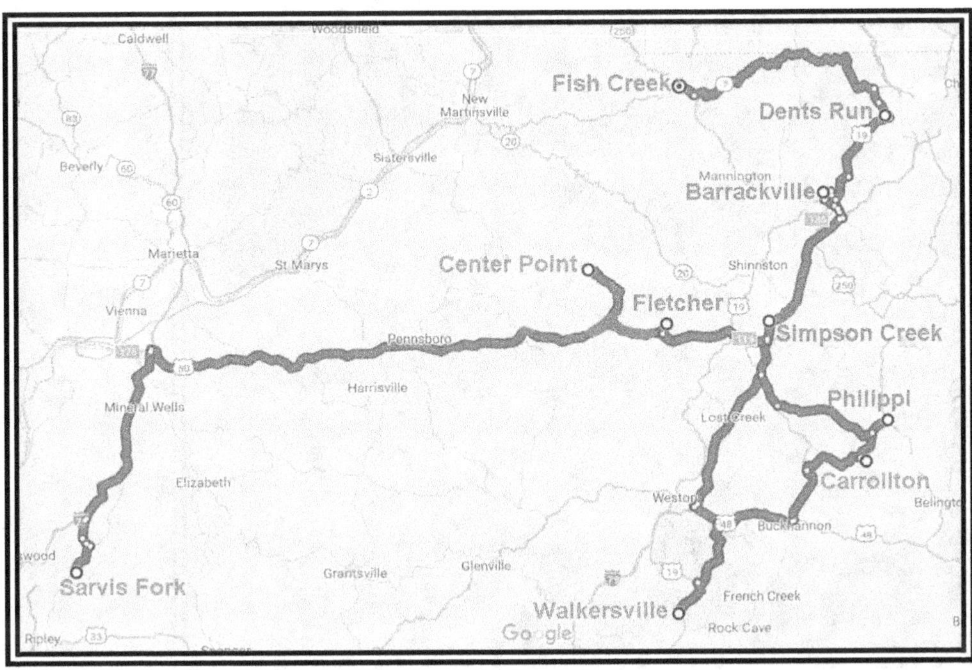

This tour covers 10 bridges and involves about 6 hours 45 minutes driving

Sarvis Fork Covered Bridge	N 38° 55.294' W 81° 38.697'
Center Point Covered Bridge	N 39° 23.384' W 80° 38.051'
Walkersville Covered Bridge	N 38° 51.511' W 80° 27.615'
Carrollton Covered Bridge	N 39° 05.423' W 80° 05.220'
Philippi Covered Bridge	N 39° 09.217' W 80° 02.561'
Simpson Creek Covered Bridge	N 39° 18.499' W 80° 16.763'
Fletcher Covered Bridge	N 39° 18.319' W 80° 28.823'
Barrackville Covered Bridge	N 39° 30.340' W 80° 10.077'
Dents Run Covered Bridge	N 39° 37.432' W 80° 02.452'
Fish Creek Covered Bridge	N 39° 40.363' W 80° 27.122'

West Virginia Tour2

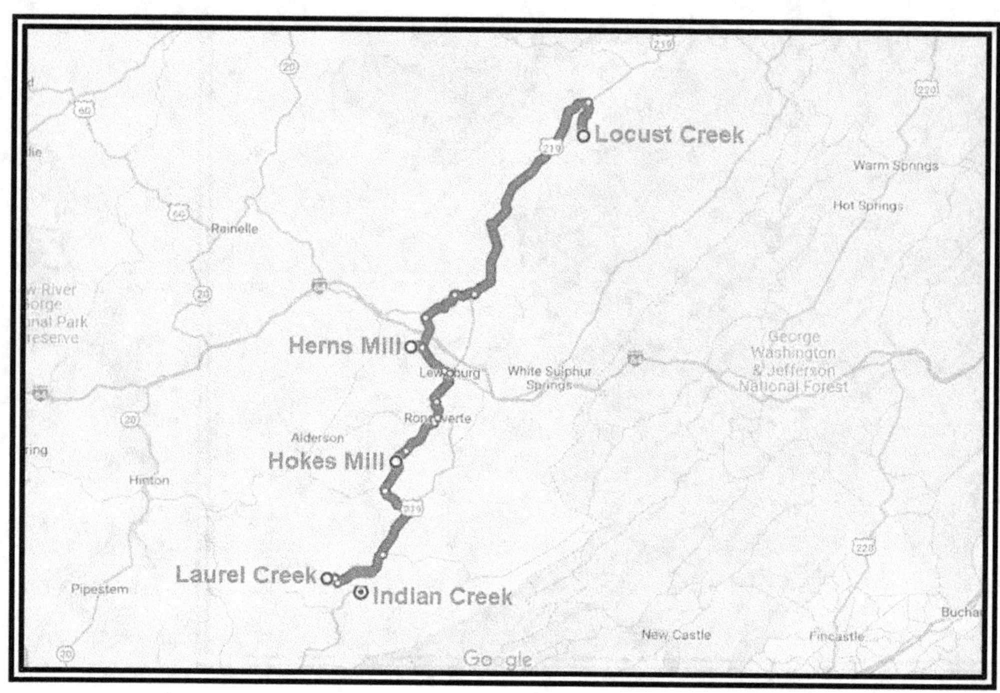

This tour covers 5 bridges and involves about 2 hours driving

Locust Creek Covered Bridge	N 38° 04.754' W 80° 14.992'
Herns Mill Covered Bridge	N 37° 49.951' W 80° 30.263'
Hokes Mill Covered Bridge	N 37° 41.871' W 80° 31.517'
Laurel Creek Covered Bridge	N 37° 33.680' W 80° 37.573'
Indian Creek Covered Bridge	N 37° 32.814' W 80° 34.498'

Recently Lost
The following bridges have been lost since 2000

Bob White Covered Bridge

Alabama
Oakachoy or Thomas Covered Bridge, AL/01-19-01x, Burned July 2001
Lidy Walker or Big Branch Covered Bridge, AL/01-22-12x, Collapsed 2001
Salem or Shotwell or Pea Ridge Covered Bridge, AL/01-41-04x, Collapsed June 4, 2005

Georgia
Wehadkee Creek (Callaway Gardens) Covered Bridge, GA/10-72-01x, Placed in storage February 2022

Kentucky
Beech Fork or Mt. Zion or Mooresville Covered Bridge, KY/17-115-01x, Lost to Arson March 9, 2021
Valley Pike (Bouldin, Daugherty) Covered Bridge, KY/17-81-02x, Lost to flood April 27, 2018
Tennessee
Port Royal Covered Bridge, TN/42-63-01#4x, Demolished October 2008

Virginia
Bob White (Lower) Covered Bridge, VA/46-68-01x, Destroyed by flood, September 29, 2015
C.K. Reynolds (Red Maple) Covered Bridge, VA/46-35-03x, Destroyed by high winds, March 1, 2017

Glossary

Abutment: The abutments are the bridge supports on each side bank. Usually they were originally constructed of stone but they have often been replaced or supplemented with concrete through the years.

Arch: A curved timber or timber set which is shaped in a curve and functions as a support of the bridge.

Bed timbers: Timbers between the abutment and the truss or bottom chord.

Brace or bracing: A diagonal timber or timber set used to support the trusses.

Bridge Deck: The roadway through the bridge.

Buttress: Wood or metal members on the exterior sides which connect the floor beams and the top of the truss. Used to keep the bridge structure from twisting under wind, water and snow loads.

Camber: A planned curve in the structure to compensate for the weight of the structure.

Chord: The horizontal members extending the length of the truss meant to carry the load to the abutments.

Dead load: The load of the weight of the bridge itself.

Deck: The pathway through the bridge used by pedestrians or vehicles.

Pier: Stone/concrete supports built in the stream bed to support the bridge

Portal: The bridge's entrances.

Post: The truss's vertical members.

Span: The bridge length measured between the abutments.

Treenails or trunnels: Pins or dowels turned from hardwood, driven into holes drilled into the members of the truss to hold them together. Also used in mortised joints.

Truss: The framework which carries the load of the bridge and distributes it to the abutments.

Truss Types

A Truss is a system of ties and struts which are connected to act like a single beam to distribute and carry a load. In covered bridges, these Trusses carry the load to stone abutments at each side and perhaps piers in between. Following are the most common types of Trusses used in Covered Bridges.

Kingpost
Kingpost is the simplest form of Truss with two diagonal members on a bottom chord, often with a vertical post connecting to the diagonals.
The multiple Kingpost involves a series of Kingposts symmetrical from the bridges center. This allows for a much longer span.

Queenpost
The Queenpost has the peak of the kingpost type replaced with a horizontal top chord which allows for a longer span.

Long

The Long Truss was patented by Stephen Long in 1830. It is a series of X shaped diagonals connected to vertical posts.

Burr Arch

Invented in 1804 by Theodore Burr, the Burr Arch is one of the most commonly found structures in Covered Bridge design. It is often used in combination with multiple kingposts. The ends of the arch are buried in the abutments.

Howe Truss

Howe

The Howe Truss was patented in 1840 by William Howe. It involves the use of vertical metal rods between the joints of wooden diagonals.

Town Truss

Town

The Town or lattice system was patented by Ithiel Town in 1820. It involved a system of overlapping diagonals in a lattice pattern connected at the intersection by Tree nails or trunnels, wooden pegs or dowels. It had the advantages in that it could be constructed by unskilled labor and local materials could be used.

Childs

Childs

The Childs Truss System is essentially a multiple kingpost with half of the diagonal timbers replaced with iron bars.

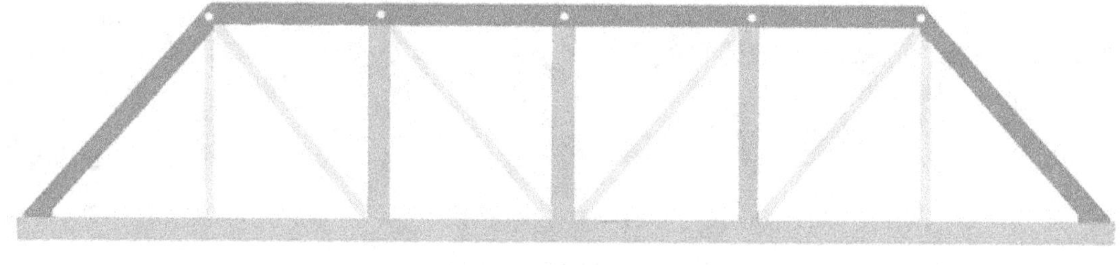

Pratt

Pratt

The Pratt truss was patented in 1844 by Caleb Pratt and his son Thomas Willis Pratt. The design uses vertical members for compression and horizontal members to respond to tension.

Smith
Robert W. Smith received patents in 1867 and 1869 for variations of his system.

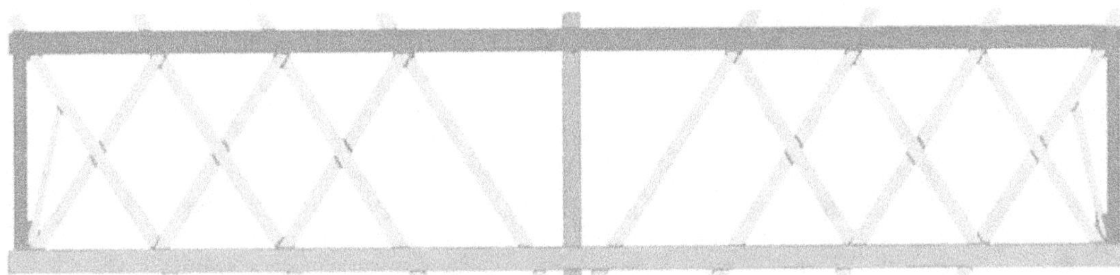

Partridge
Reuben L. Partridge received a patent for a design similar to the Smith system but adding terminal braces at the end and a central vertical member.

Warren

Warren

Patented in 1848 by two Englishmen, one of whom was named James Warren, it consists of parallel upper and lower chords with diagonal connecting members forming a series of equilateral triangles.

Paddleford

Paddleford

Peter Paddleford worked with the Long Truss system and eventually adapted it with a system of interlocking braces. he was never able to patent the system due to challenges from the owners of the Long Truss patent. However there are a number of New Hampshire and Vermont bridges which use the Paddleford system

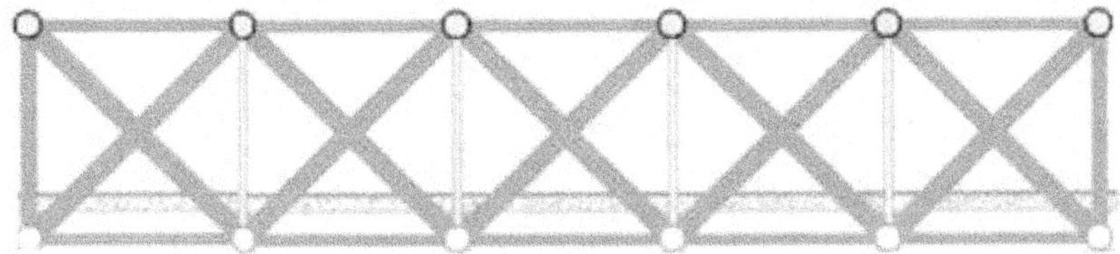

Brown

Brown

Josiah Brown Jr., of Buffalo, New York, patented this system in 1857.It consists of diagonal cross compression members connected to horizontal top and bottom stringers and is known for economic use of materials. It was only used in Michigan where there are a couple of surviving members.

References

National Society for the Preservation of Covered Bridges
http://www.coveredbridgesociety.org

New York State Covered Bridge Society
http://www.nycoveredbridges.org

Vermont Covered Bridge Society
http://www.vermontbridges.com/

Covered Bridge Society of Oregon
http://www.covered-bridges.org/

The Theodore Burr Covered Bridge Society of Pennsylvania
http://www.tbcbspa.com/

Indiana Covered Bridge Society
http://www.indianacrossings.org/

Ohio Historic Bridge Association
http://oldohiobridges.com/ohba/index.htm

Harold Stiver Image Gallery
https://haroldstiver.smugmug.com/Galleries/Themes/Covered-Bridges

Photo Credits:

Alabama Covered Bridges
All images by the author

Georgia Covered Bridges
TC2U, *Lulu;* **Jerrye & Roy Klotz MD,** *Coheelee Creek*
All other images by the author

Kentucky Covered Bridges
All images by the author

Missouri Covered Bridges
Parker Botanical, *Bollinger Mill Covered Bridge*
All other images by the author

Tennessee Covered Bridges
All images by the author

Virginia Covered Bridges
All images by the author

West Virginia Covered Bridges
All images by the author

The Photographer's and Explorer's Series

Unless noted, there are Print and eBook editions available for the following.

Birding Guide to Orkney
Guide to Photographing Birds
Maine Lighthouses
Ontario Lighthouses
Ontario's Old Mills
Ontario Waterfalls

Alabama Covered Bridges (eBook)
California Covered Bridges (eBook)
Connecticut Covered Bridges (eBook)
Georgia Covered Bridges (eBook)
Indiana Covered Bridges
Maine Covered Bridges (eBook)
Massachusetts Covered Bridges (eBook)
Michigan Covered Bridges (eBook)
New Brunswick Covered Bridges
New England Covered Bridges
Covered Bridges of the Mid-Atlantic
Covered Bridges of the South
New Hampshire Covered Bridges
New York Covered Bridges
Ohio's Covered Bridges
The Covered Bridges of Kentucky (eBook)
The Covered Bridges of Kentucky and Tennessee
The Covered Bridges of Tennessee (eBook)
Vermont's Covered Bridges
The Covered Bridges of Virginia (eBook)
The Covered Bridges of Virginia and West Virginia
Washington Covered Bridges (eBook)
The Covered Bridges of West Virginia (eBook)
West Coast Covered Bridges

Index

Kentucky Index

Missouri Index